MODERN
CIDER

MODERN
CIDER

**Simple recipes to make your
own ciders, perries, cysers, shrubs,
fruit wines, vinegars & more**

EMMA CHRISTENSEN

**Photographs by
Kelly Puleio**

TEN SPEED PRESS
California | New York

contents

introduction

I made and bottled my inaugural cider almost six years ago while working on my first book, *True Brews*. Up to that point, my association with ciders had been fairly limited to the cheap variety served to shy freshmen like myself at parties in college, which tasted nearly identical to the stuff served to five-year-olds except it was fizzier and tended to make us giggly. I wasn't sure what to expect from my homemade version, but I was fairly sure I could at least achieve giggle-status.

But then my first cider absolutely blew me away. It was bright and effervescent, boozy but sophisticated, tart but tempered with the lingering sweetness of late-summer apples. This was definitely a cider for grown-ups, fully deserving of a pint glass and not a sippy cup.

Perhaps even more surprising, this cider was incredibly easy to make. I picked up a gallon of apple juice at the store, added yeast and a few other ingredients from my brew kit, and left it to do its fermentation business in the corner for a few weeks. As a homebrewer, I'm used to reserving whole afternoons to making batches of beer, and as a winemaker, I'm accustomed to months of wait time before wine becomes drinkable. Compared to this, making cider felt like cheating. Delicious cheating.

The wheels in my head started to turn. If I could make cider this good with basic store-bought juice, what could I make with actual heirloom cider apples? What about fresh juice from a local orchard? Or even (if I dared) the mass-market stuff served to five-year-olds?

That was the beginning. This book is a map of where I've traveled in the years since.

what is cider?

In the simplest, most basic definition, cider is fermented apple juice. In the United States, we've gotten our terms for alcoholic and nonalcoholic cider somewhat confused over the decades, so we usually refer to alcoholic cider as "hard cider" while everyone else in the world just calls it "cider." In this book, we'll follow the global crowd for our terminology: alcoholic fermented apple juice is "cider"; unfermented apple juice is simply "juice."

True cider, like the kind you make yourself or get from a good craft cidery, is very different from the mass-market cider you may be used to. For one thing, it's typically not very sweet. It can be tart, sour, balanced, funky, mellow, spicy, dry, bitter, apple-y, or wine-like, but it's generally *not* what most of us would consider sweet. True cider isn't even always fizzy; many traditional ciders are actually served still (that is, nonsparkling or nonfizzy).

If you, like me, spent your college years drinking cider that was as sweet as candy and as fizzy as soda, then you'll need to retrain your taste buds. I recommend a cider tasting to get a feel for what you're about to make. Head to a well-stocked liquor store and pick up a few different bottles. Get a mix of US craft ciders and imported ciders, if you can. Then invite a few curious friends over to your place and start opening bottles. You'll quickly get an idea of what the wide world of ciders has to offer—and what tasty rewards are in your future when you make your own.

how cider is made

All cider starts with juice. How and where you get this juice, its quality, its particular characteristics, and its balance of flavors—these are all factors that go into your finished cider. You don't have to seek out fancy heirloom apples just to make good cider, but you do need to put some thought into the juice you're using. We'll go into this in much more detail in chapter 1, Turning Apples into Juice. For now, just be assured that no matter what apples or juice you have available, you can definitely make a tasty cider. No doubt about it.

Once you have some juice, turning it into cider is the easy part. Fresh-pressed juice is so full of natural sugars and wild yeasts that you can practically see it start to ferment in front of your eyes. Even pasteurized, store-bought juice has plenty of sugar to ferment; you just need to add some yeast purchased at a homebrew store.

The yeast eats up the sugar and gives you alcohol and carbon dioxide in return. In a few weeks, you'll have homemade cider—it really is just about as simple as that! In chapter 2, Setting Up Your Cider House, we'll go over all the equipment and extra ingredients you need to make a good cider, and then in chapter 3, Turning Juice into Cider, we'll go over this whole cider-making process in greater detail.

making a modern cider

People have been turning apples into cider for almost as long as there have been apple trees, so what is "modern" cider? This is cider making tailored to a new generation of cider drinkers. It's cider made in tiny third-floor walk-ups, sunny country kitchens, and suburban garages with the door rolled up. It's cider that uses what you have on hand, whether that's picking up a gallon of fresh juice at the farmers' market, using your juicer to juice your own apples, or cruising the pantry aisle at the grocery store for some bottled stuff. It's cider on a scale that works for you—small 1-gallon experiments or larger 5-gallon batches to share with friends. It's cider made with hops, or with fresh pineapple, or with bourbon. Modern cider is your cider; it's whatever you want it to be.

Start with the recipes in chapter 4, Beginner Ciders. These are "low-risk, high-reward" recipes that will help you master the basics of turning apple juice into cider. Next, chapter 5, The Cider Family, will introduce you to two close cousins to apple cider. These are "perries," ciders made with pear juice, and "cysers," ciders made with honey.

The party really starts when we get to chapter 6, Modern Ciders, and chapter 7, Ciders for Beer Lovers. The recipes in these two chapters bring ingredients like hops, rum-soaked oak cubes, and fresh summer berries into play to make some truly modernized ciders. When

getting to know ciders

GOAL

To familiarize yourself with the range and variety of ciders.

WHAT YOU NEED

Five to eight different bottles of cider. Stick with plain apple cider (no crazy flavors for now) and try to get a mix of ciders from large commercial cider makers, small craft cider makers, and North American and European cider makers.

WHAT TO DO

Pour a small amount of each cider into clear tumblers of the same size. Lift each one up to the light and make note of the color and clarity. Smell each cider and then take a small sip. Let it roll across your tongue before swallowing.

Take notes about the aromas and flavors that you notice, how the cider physically feels on your tongue, and whether it leaves your mouth feeling dry, clean tasting, or sticky. Do any of these things change on your second sip, or your third? What characteristics you like? What do you *not* like?

There are no wrong answers here. Just taste your way through and take notes as you go. This is about exposing yourself to a range of different ciders and starting to get a feel for the different aromas and flavors in each one. You're putting your first entries into your mental encyclopedia of cider characteristics.

EXTRA CREDIT

Repeat this tasting with just European ciders, or just North American ciders, or even just the ciders from one particular cider maker.

you need to take a break and just want something quick and sparkly to drink, give the nonalcoholic and low-alcohol drinks from chapter 8, Soft Ciders, a try.

Take your cider to the other end of the spectrum with the recipes in chapter 9, Apple Wines. These table wines, champagnes, and dessert wines build on the same methods used throughout the book, but push your cider in a much boozier direction. And last but not least, chapter 10, Traditional Ciders, takes a look at the cider traditions of England, France, Spain, and the United States. These recipes are more advanced, so save them until you have a few of the more basic recipes under your belt before trying. They're great fun when you have a surplus of apples to use up and some time to experiment.

is making cider safe?

Most of the concerns about cider safety are from unpasteurized, unfermented raw apple juice. Once fermented, the risk for food-borne illness is very small—the low pH along with the alcohol content in fermented cider are enough to kill *E. coli*, *Salmonella*, and all other common illness-causing bacteria.

Even so, it's always a smart idea to practice good sanitation and follow food safety guidelines when making cider. If you're pressing fresh apples, make sure to wash the apples and cut away any blemishes before pressing. Sanitize all equipment that comes into contact with the cider at every stage in the process, including jugs, caps, and bottles.

Use your best judgment if you think a batch of cider has picked up an infection somewhere along the way. You'll know when this happens because the cider will smell spoiled, look slimy, or have mold on the surface. An infected batch of cider isn't likely to make you seriously ill, but it's always better to be safe than sorry—and who wants to drink bad cider anyway? Life is too short for that.

is making cider legal?

Good news! Making your own cider is legal in all fifty states in the United States, though you'll need to limit your obsession to 100 gallons of cider, beer, or wine per adult, or 200 gallons per household, each calendar year. If you hit that limit, then it's probably time to open a cidery and go pro.

By the way, you'll also need to open a cidery if you want to start selling your cider—you can trade it, gift it, or hoard it all in your basement, but selling homemade cider is against the law without the proper licenses.

let's make some cider

Above all, with this book and these recipes, I want you to have some fun. Making cider isn't hard—apples practically *want* to ferment into cider. You're just assisting in the natural course of events, guiding them toward the best and tastiest outcome. Consider it a favor to apples everywhere.

What are you waiting for? Let's make some cider.

turning apples into juice

Apples are amazing. These round, rosy-hued fruits contain pretty much everything you need to make a fine batch of cider, from the juice that ultimately becomes the cider to the sugars needed to feed the yeast to all the various acids, tannins, and flavor compounds that give cider its great flavor. Fresh, unpasteurized apple juice even has its own wild yeast population, ready and waiting!

Now, this doesn't mean that you need to live next door to an apple orchard in order to make your own cider. There are many ways to get your hands on some apple juice: you can press your own apples or juice them with a juicer, you can buy raw or pasteurized juice from the farmers' market, or you can pick up a few gallons of juice on your next trip to the supermarket. Generally speaking, the closer you can come to getting your juice fresh from the source (the apple itself), the better your cider will ultimately be, but you can still make a darn good cider with any juice you use.

We'll get more deeply into the "how" of making cider in the next few chapters. But first, let's spend some time focusing on where it all begins: the apples and their juice.

the three main types of apples

For our cider-making purposes, there are three big, overarching categories for apples: sweet apples, acidic apples, and bitter apples. You might hear them go by different names depending on whom you're talking to and where that person is from, but I find that it's most useful to think about apples in terms of what they bring to the party, cider-wise. Sweet apples bring most of the sugar to feed the yeast, acidic apples bring the tart flavors, and bitter apples bring some tannins and body to the cider. All three kinds of apples provide apple-icious flavors and aromas. Combined, these apples will give you a balanced cider with a nice complexity of flavors and aromas in the glass.

SWEET APPLES

Sweet apples are familiar to most of us from grocery store displays and school lunches. These apples, like Gala, Fuji, and Golden Delicious, are great to eat on their own. They taste sweet and juicy with a nice apple-y perfume and maybe a touch of tartness. Don't be fooled by the term "sweet." It doesn't necessarily refer to high sugar, but rather to low tannin and acid content. In the apple-growing and cider-making industries, these are also called "dessert apples" or "eating apples."

These apples are packed with sugar, but this doesn't actually mean your cider will end up tasting sugary or sweet. All that sugar is really just food for the yeast, and the yeast keeps eating until all the sugar is gone. Since sweet apples have a fairly reliable amount of sugar, think of these apples as your base. You'll want a good amount of them in your juice in order to make a good batch. A larger portion of sweet apples, or using apples with particularly high amounts of natural sugar, will also make a boozier cider.

A good, and very easy, rule of thumb when you're buying sweet apples is to choose apples that taste good to you. Besides bringing the food for the yeast, sweet apples also add some great flavors and aromas to the cider, so try to look beyond the simple sweetness of the apple and choose ones that have interesting flavor and character.

ACIDIC APPLES

Acidic apples are often known as "cooking apples," "culinary apples," or "pie apples." Cider makers also usually refer to them as "sharps." These apples are more tart than sweet, like Granny Smith, McIntosh, and Mutsu varieties. Some are nice to eat by the slice, but their sweet-tart flavor and firm texture are also fantastic for making irresistible apple pies, cobblers, and tarts—and cider.

These apples add some sugar to the cider, but mostly they bring bright, tart, acidic flavors. Without a good dose of this sharpness, your cider would taste bland and boring. Acidic apples perk up the party.

Just as with sweet apples, you can usually go by taste when buying acidic apples. If it makes your mouth pucker at least a little bit, then it will probably work well in your cider.

BITTER APPLES

When professional cider makers talk about "cider apples," it's this group of bitter apples that they mean. These apples are so hard, bitter, and astringent that you'll wonder why anyone ever thought they'd be useful for anything except composting. Take a bite and you'll immediately spit it out—which is why they're also called "spitters"!

But these apples play a key role in making a good cider. They bring in some sugar and acidity, but mostly they add tannins, like those found in a rich red wine or in a mug of tea left to steep for a little too long. Tannins can be perceived both as bitterness and as a physical sensation, like roughness or dryness in your mouth. A cider with the right amount of tannin won't scream it from the rooftops, but you'll notice that it tastes a little fuller in your mouth and more complex in flavor than those without.

Since most commercial orchards have been fully converted to growing primarily sweet or acidic apples, bitter apples can be hard to find. Your best bet for getting your hands on some is to talk to an apple grower from a nearby orchard; there's a decent chance he or she has a few old gnarled cider apple trees growing somewhere in the orchard. Crabapples and quinces also serve nicely as "cider apples" and

the economics
of buying apples

One major factor to consider when buying apples is their cost. Apples are not always cheap, and the heirloom varieties of apples that make a truly great cider can come with a truly great price tag. It's good to think through the economics before getting too carried away with plans for a new cider.

I like to calculate the price per bottle of my potential cider and compare that to the price per bottle of a high-end cider that I could buy at the store. If the price per bottle is roughly the same, then I'm happy. That means I'm at least breaking even on my budget. If the price per bottle of my homemade cider is significantly greater, then I give it some real thought before I commit.

Let's say a six-pack of good-quality cider at the store costs roughly $10. This makes the cost per bottle about $1.60.

If the apples I'm interested in using are $2.99 a pound and I need about 20 pounds to make a gallon of juice, that means a 1-gallon batch of cider will cost me about $60. This makes roughly ten 12-ounce bottles, so the cost per bottle is about $6.60. For me, this cost is too high and I'd need a very compelling reason to make this cider. By contrast, if the apples are $1 per pound, then that comes out to $20 for the gallon and $2.20 per bottle. This gets me a little more in the ballpark for a financially feasible project.

This same logic works for buying apple juice, too. A gallon of really amazing, fresh-pressed, organic apple juice from a local orchard that costs $12 a gallon might seem expensive, but it actually comes out to $1.30 a bottle. Not bad for good-quality juice!

Ideally, I like to buy apples that are less than $1 per pound or juice that is less than $15 per gallon. I also still have to buy yeast, enzymes, and other ingredients, but their cost is relatively small in comparison to the apples and less of a factor in the overall economics of cider making at home.

can be a little easier to find. As cider becomes more popular, hopefully we'll start seeing more kinds of cider apples available to us at farmers' markets and local orchards.

Don't get too hung up on finding these bitter apples. They're great if you can get them, but you can still make good cider without them. In the next chapter, we'll talk about some ways to doctor your cider if you think it could use some extra tannins.

blending apples for the perfect juice

Very few apples have everything it takes to make a good cider. This means that the best juice for cider is usually made from a blend of several different kinds of apples. In fact, the more apples, the merrier! Every apple has its own unique flavors and character, and cider made from blended juice will be more complex, flavorful, and memorable than one made from just one or two varieties.

A good place to start when making your own blended apple juice is to use 30 to 60 percent sweet apples, 10 to 20 percent acidic apples, and 5 to 20 percent bitter apples. This makes a juice with a solid base of sugars (which feed the yeast, remember) along with bright acidity and a touch of dry, tannic astringency.

Apples are usually categorized by their dominant trait—sweet, acidic, or bitter—but most will have some overlapping characteristics. For example, a McIntosh apple is mostly tart, but also has a good amount of sugar. A Gravenstein apple is acidic, but also adds some bitterness. Apples can also differ from season to season, or even from the start of the season to the end, so let your taste buds be your ultimate guide.

Blending apples as a home cider maker is less about precision and more about trusting your instincts. Taste apples before buying them, if you can, and use your best judgment about how much of each to use in your blend. As long as you're using a good mix of apples, you'll usually end up with something interesting.

If you're buying your juice rather than pressing it yourself, most of this work of blending has already been done for you. You're not likely going to know what specific apples went into the juice blend, but you can still get a good sense of the balance just by taking a sip and tasting it. Ideally, the juice should taste sweet and a little tart with a rich apple flavor. You can also blend juices together to achieve a better balance.

What if you're not sure? Go ahead and ferment it! You can always adjust the flavor balance before bottling with the tricks we'll talk about in chapter 3, Turning Juice into Cider.

where to get your juice

This is the million-dollar question, isn't it? Maybe you don't live near an orchard with dozens of varieties of apples to choose from. Maybe you do live near an orchard, but you don't have any way of juicing the apples once you get them home. Or maybe they're really expensive and making a batch of cider starts looking cost prohibitive. Maybe you're craving cider in the middle of May and apple season is still months away. Maybe you just don't want to bother with all this picking and pressing nonsense, and you'd rather just get straight to the part where you make cider.

Cider is not a one-size-fits-all operation. We all have our own situations and our own goals when it comes to cider making. Whatever those things look like for you, there is a juice that's going to work. The following sections cover my top four ways of getting your hands on some apple juice, starting with the freshest option and finishing with ideas for when apples or fresh juice are hard to find.

APPLES TO JUICE AMOUNTS

18 TO 20 POUNDS (8.2 TO 9.1 KG) APPLES = 1 GALLON PRESSED JUICE

90 TO 100 POUNDS (40.8 TO 45.4 KG, OR ABOUT 2 BUSHELS) APPLES = 5 GALLONS PRESSED JUICE

apples for cider

	SWEET	ACIDIC	BITTER
ALSO CALLED	Dessert apples, eating apples	Cooking apples, culinary apples, pie apples, sharp apples	Cider apples, bittersharp apples (high tannin, high acid), bittersweet apples (high tannin, low acid), "spitters"
% TOTAL JUICE BLEND	30 to 60 percent	10 to 20 percent	5 to 20 percent
GENERAL CHARACTERISTICS	High sugar, low to medium acidity, low tannin	High acidity, medium to high sugar, low tannin	High tannin, low to high acidity, low to medium sugar
HOW TO RECOGNIZE	Sweet and juicy, great for eating on their own	Very tart and acidic, but often with some sweetness; some are good to eat on their own, but they're usually saved for pies and other desserts	Generally too bitter and hard to eat; they make your mouth taste dry and fuzzy
WHAT IT BRINGS TO THE CIDER	Sugar (for the yeast), apple aroma, some apple flavor	Acidic brightness, apple aroma, some apple flavor	Dry, tannic astringency; fuller mouthfeel
COMMON VARIETIES	Fuji, Gala, Rome, Empire, Golden Delicious, Red Delicious, Jonagold, Honeycrisp, Braeburn, Jonathan, Golden Russet, Roxbury Russett	Baldwin, Newtown Pippin, McIntosh, Black Oxford, Northern Spy, Granny Smith, Gravenstein, Mutsu/Crispin, Arkansas Black, Ashmead's Kernel, Winesap, Cortland	Dabinett, Nehou, Kingston Black, Stoke Red, crabapple (any variety), quince (any variety)

CIDER LESSON 2
getting to know apples

GOAL
To understand the range of apples and apple flavors.

WHAT YOU NEED
Five to ten different varieties of apples.

WHAT TO DO
Slice off a small piece of each apple and taste one at a time. Hold the slice up to your nose and see if you can smell any aromas. Take a bite of the flesh by itself, and then a bite of the flesh with some peel. Chew it thoroughly and press the apple against your tongue before swallowing.

As you do all of this, try to notice the different flavors in the apple. Is it mostly sweet? Does the sweetness remind you of anything—like vanilla or spring flowers or honey? Is the acidity sharp tasting or fairly mellow? Is it sour? Does this flavor overwhelm the sweetness or balance it? Does the apple taste bitter or leave your mouth tasting dry after you swallow (a sign of tannins)?

After you go through the whole lineup, go back and try tasting two different apples together. Pair a sweet apple with an acidic apple, or with a bitter apple.

This is the first step to understanding how to blend apples into an ideal juice for your cider. Try to think beyond your initial instinct of "like" or "dislike," and instead think about how these apples blend together. By tasting lots of different apples, your brain starts to catalog the flavors, and you will gradually make associations between the apples and the qualities in a finished cider.

EXTRA CREDIT
Go to the farmers' market and get one apple of the same variety from several different orchards. What is similar and different about each one?

PRESS YOUR OWN APPLES

You'll need about 20 pounds of apples to make 1 gallon of cider, and around 100 pounds (about 2 bushels) to make 5 gallons of cider. Go ahead and mix all your different apples together before juicing, crushing, or pressing. Mixing is especially important when crushing bitter apples, crabapples, or quinces, which are very hard and dense and don't crush very well on their own.

Make sure all the apples are clean and thoroughly rinsed of any detergents. Trim away any large, obvious bruises or blemishes, but small nicks or shallow bruises are fine. Assemble your equipment and make sure it is clean, though there's no need to sanitize the equipment for this step. Have buckets or jugs ready for collecting the pressed juice.

For small amounts of apples (less than 20 pounds), I like to use an electric juicer. Juicers are very good at extracting all the available liquid from the apple solids, and you often get a higher yield of juice than you do with an apple press. To use one, you will generally want to cut away the stems and cores from your apples, but there's no need to peel. Cut the apples into a size that will fit into the mouth of your juicer. Feed the apples into the juicer, collect the juice at the other end, and you're done. Every juicer is a little different, so check the instructions before using.

For larger amounts of apples (more than 20 pounds), it's better to use an apple press. This allows you to process more apples at once, which is ultimately more time and energy efficient—plus you avoid the risk of blowing out the motor on your juicer! Along with the press itself, you'll also need a fruit crusher for grinding the apples into a pulp (that is, "pomace").

These apple presses and crushers are a big investment, so do your research and think through your needs carefully before buying one. Many homebrew shops rent fruit presses by the day, which is a great option if you're not ready to invest in your own. (When shopping for presses, note that apple presses, fruit presses, and wine presses are all the same thing. For reference, I used a Weston Fruit & Apple Crusher and a Weston Wine Press when working on this book.)

Pressing apples is a two-part process. First, you grind the apples into a mashed and shredded pomace using the fruit crusher, then you press the pomace in the apple press to extract the juice. No need to stem or core apples when using a crusher, but the process is a little easier if you cut the apples into halves or quarters. Most crushers have a big drum with barbed metal teeth, which you turn using a crank. Feed the apples through the top, turn the crank, and shredded apples come out the bottom. Be sure you have a bucket or other big receptacle ready to catch the pomace.

You might be wondering if you can pulverize your apples in a blender instead of a fancy fruit crusher. It's possible, but personally, I don't recommend it. Fruit crushers work by shredding apples instead of fully pulverizing them, so you're left with a chunky mash with a good amount of solid material. Most blenders and food processors will break down the apples a little too thoroughly and that makes it difficult to separate the liquids from the solids during pressing. You wind up with a lot of sediment in your juice.

Once you've mashed your apples into a pomace, you're ready to press the juice. All presses work in basically the same way: fill it up and press! I recommend lining the inside of the press with a large mesh fruit bag (available at homebrewing stores) to help filter out as much sediment as possible and keep the pomace nicely contained. Before you pour the pomace into the press, make sure you have a bucket ready to catch the juice; grinding releases a lot of juice on its own, so the juice will start flowing as soon as you pour the pomace into the press.

Keep pressing until the flow of juice starts to slow and it becomes difficult to press any further. Once you get to this point, take a break and let the pomace finish draining on its own for a few minutes. Once no more juice is flowing, remove the pomace from the press, and discard or compost it. The press and crusher can both be cleaned using soap and water and left to air dry.

Each fruit crusher and apple press has its own particular quirks, so be sure to read all instructions thoroughly before you start. The first time you

use your press, set aside a few hours on a weekend afternoon to give yourself time to get used to the new equipment.

Fresh-pressed juice will keep refrigerated for a day or two, but it's best to get started on the cider as soon as you can to avoid any spoilage or chance that the wild yeast in the juice will get a jump start on fermentation—unless, of course, you actually *want* the wild yeast to get started (see chapter 10, Traditional Ciders, for more on that topic). You can also freeze fresh-pressed juice for several months without any significant change in flavor or deterioration in quality.

Fresh-pressed juice does not need to be pasteurized or otherwise treated before using it to make cider. For some recipes, I recommend treating the juice with Campden tablets (potassium metabisulfite) to minimize the risk of spoilage and competition from wild yeast before using it to make cider. See page 40 for more on this topic.

FRESH-PRESSED JUICE FROM AN ORCHARD

Second best to juice you've pressed yourself is buying juice that has been freshly pressed for you by someone else. Many orchards press their own juice in small batches throughout the autumn harvest season and sell it directly to consumers at farm stands and farmers' markets. Some orchards also have arrangements with nearby homebrew stores to sell bulk juice to customers in the fall months. Check with your local store to see if this is an option for you.

This fresh-from-the-orchard juice is typically sold raw (unpasteurized) or only very minimally pasteurized. This means that all (or most) of the delicate flavors and aromas from the apples are preserved in the juice and will eventually make their way into your cider. Since the juice is usually pressed from whatever apples are being harvested at the time, you're also getting a snapshot of the season and the local microclimate—you're about to make a cider that no one else will ever get to taste and that will never be quite the same again!

Fresh juice from orchards is usually bottled and sold within a few days of pressing, though some orchards will freeze jugs until they can make it to a market. (Freezing does not affect the flavor or overall quality of the juice.) Keep fresh juice refrigerated and plan to make your cider within a few days of purchase, or freeze it until you're ready to make cider.

If the juice you purchased is raw and unpasteurized, it can be used as is and does not need to be pasteurized or otherwise treated before being used to make cider. For some recipes, I recommend treating the juice with Campden tablets (potassium metabisulfite) to minimize the risk of spoilage and competition from wild yeast before using it to make cider. See page 40 for more on this topic.

BOTTLED JUICE FROM THE REFRIGERATOR SECTION

Your next best bet for juice is looking in the refrigerator section at the grocery store. This juice is usually pressed and processed in large batches at industrial facilities and has almost always been pasteurized to extend its shelf life.

Look for juices that have been flash-pasteurized, "lightly" pasteurized, or "high temperature short time" (HTST) pasteurized. This indicates a less intense form of pasteurization; you still lose some character and complexity in the juice, but less so than with other forms of pasteurization. This juice is also typically much more affordable than buying apples or fresh juice (often less than $10 a gallon) and it can still be used to make a very good cider, especially if you use some of the extra cider-making tricks we talk about in the next few chapters.

There is a big spectrum in flavor and quality with these refrigerated store-bought juices, from blandly sweet to nicely tart and well balanced. Look for bottles that are not from concentrate, have not had any sugar added, and contain no preservatives. The words "fresh-pressed" on the label is virtually meaningless in this context, but refrigerated juices tend to be fresher than the heavily pasteurized ones you find in the pantry aisle. Cloudy, unfiltered juice (sometimes labeled "cider") tends to be more nuanced and flavorful than crystal clear, filtered juice. If you can, buy a small jug of whatever juice you're thinking of using and sample it before you start your cider project.

I relied heavily on the "fresh" flash-pasteurized apple juice from Trader Joe's when developing the recipes for

pasteurization and apple juice

Pasteurization is a process that kills all yeast and bacteria in apple juice, harmful or otherwise. This is done to make the juice absolutely safe for mass-market consumption and also to extend the juice's shelf life from a mere few days to weeks, months, or even years. The process involves heating the apple juice to a specific temperature and then holding it at that temperature for a specified period of time.

On the upside, if you're making cider with pasteurized juice, you have a clean slate for your cider making. You'll have no latent yeast or bacteria to compete with those that you want to introduce yourself. You have complete artistic control. You also don't need to worry about any spoilage-causing bacteria that might ruin a good batch of cider before it has a chance to get going.

On the downside, pasteurization destroys a lot of what makes apple juice—and the resulting cider—unique, nuanced, and, in a very literal way, alive. Many of the juice's more delicate flavors and aromas are lost once it is heated, leaving you with a juice with less overall character. Pasteurization also kills all the naturally occurring wild yeast in the cider, and a wild-fermented cider is a beautiful thing. It creates a cider with a distinct terroir, a "sense of place" from where the apples were grown.

On a purely technical level, you can use either raw (unpasteurized) or pasteurized apple juice to make cider. The yeast is only interested in the sugars in the juice, and these remain largely unaffected by the pasteurization process. The choice between raw or pasteurized juice comes down to three things: personal preference, the type of cider you want to make, and the juice that is available to you.

If you are using raw, unpasteurized juice for your cider, it does not need to be pasteurized before making cider. Raw juice can be used as is, or you can treat it with Campden tablets (potassium metabisulfite) to minimize the risk of spoilage and competition from wild yeast without affecting the flavor of the juice or finished cider. See page 40 for more on this topic.

If you're concerned about the safety of using raw apple juice, know that the fermentation process itself will destroy any harmful bacteria or toxins that might be present and prevent any others from forming. This includes *E. coli*, *Clostridium botulinum* (which causes botulism), and any other bacteria that could truly cause you harm. As long as there is any fermentation at all, you are safe.

CIDER LESSON 3
getting to know apple juice

GOAL

To explore the variety of prepared juices available to you.

WHAT YOU NEED

Buy a variety of different juices, including fresh-pressed juice from a local orchard, bottled juice from the refrigerator section at the grocery store, "gourmet" bottled juice from the pantry aisle, and mass-market bottled juice. If you can, add some juice that you press yourself from a mix of apples (see Sweet Drinking Cider on page 120).

WHAT TO DO

Pour a small amount of each juice into clear tumblers of the same size. Lift each one up to the light and make note of the color and clarity. Smell each cider and then take a small sip. Let it roll across your tongue before swallowing.

What do you notice? What aromas can you detect in each juice? What flavors? Does the juice taste predominantly sweet? If so, how would you describe the sweet flavor? Do you taste any acidity or bitterness? Does the juice taste syrupy or watery on your tongue? Do you notice any dryness after you swallow, or does it leave a film in your mouth? In what ways do the raw or lightly pasteurized juices smell or taste different from the heavily pasteurized bottled juices?

After you go through the whole lineup, go back and try tasting two different juices together. How do you like the flavor after blending?

In general, the more flavors and aromas you detect in your juice, the better your cider will be. Sometimes blending two juices together will make it better. Remember, most of that sweetness will disappear during fermentation as the yeast eats the sugar, so try to taste beyond the sweetness and pull out the underlying flavors.

EXTRA CREDIT

Keep an eye out for single-variety apple juices, often available in the fall. Try each one alone, and then try blending them together in different amounts.

this book, and I highly recommend it if you are looking for an easy, affordable juice option. This juice has a good flavor profile for making cider, is of dependable quality, and is available year-round.

Keep these juices refrigerated and use them to make cider any time before their expiration date.

BOTTLED JUICE FROM THE PANTRY AISLE

As a final option, you can buy bottles of apple juice from the juice or pantry aisle at the grocery store. This juice is made in large batches at industrial food-processing facilities, and it has been pasteurized at ultrahigh temperatures to make it shelf stable for years without needing refrigeration (UT, UHT, or UP on a label). This level of pasteurization destroys any delicate flavors or aromas that might have once existed in the juice, and you're left with a sweet but rather ho-hum apple juice. I also feel that it gives the juice a slightly cooked flavor, like applesauce.

Even so, jugs of this type juice make a surprisingly good and totally respectable cider. It might not win any fancy awards, but if your aim is just to make something pleasant to drink at the end of the day, then this will certainly hit the spot. There is a wide range of quality in these juices, as well. They all taste a little bland, but you'll notice a big difference in cider made from the cheapest and most generic mass-produced juice versus the juice from smaller producers who put a little more care and effort into their product.

It's fine if your juice contains preservatives (though you may be surprised at how few bottled juices contain chemical preservatives). Commercial yeast is hardy enough to overcome the most common preservatives and your juice will still ferment just fine.

This juice is also the most economical option when making cider, so it's good for times when you want to make a lot of cider for a big crowd, like a house party or a friend's wedding.

the final word on apple juice

In general, just use the best juice you can find or afford, and then don't lose too much sleep over it. In the next few chapters, we'll go over all of the ways you can adjust your cider if you feel like it needs a little extra boost. Even cider made from the very best juice needs some help on occasion. With a little planning and creativity, you can transform any juice into a cider you'll be proud to pour into a pint glass.

setting up your cider house

Whether it's your kitchen, your garage, or a shed out back, if you're making cider, it's your cider house. Make sure it's stocked and supplied with everything you need to make a good batch of cider.

All of the equipment and cider-making ingredients covered in this chapter are available at homebrew supply stores or online at places like MoreBeer.com and NorthernBrewer.com. If you also make beer or wine at home, you can use the same equipment for making cider.

cider-making equipment

You don't need a lot of special equipment to make cider, but a few things will make your life easier and result in better cider. None of these items is terribly expensive, but if budget is a concern, you might think about starting with 1-gallon batches. Small batches are also great if you're living in an apartment without much storage space and want to keep your cider-making operation fairly compact.

In addition to the fermentation-specific equipment covered here, there are a few everyday kitchen tools that you'll want to have nearby when making cider. These include things like pots and pans, a digital thermometer, measuring cups and spoons, a whisk, and an electronic kitchen scale.

AIR LOCK This useful little gadget lets gases escape from the vessel of fermenting cider while preventing anything else, like bacteria or fruit flies, from getting in, which might contaminate the cider. There are two main kinds of air locks: three-piece air locks and bubbler air locks. Either one is fine.

To use an air lock, fill it with a little sanitizer solution, vodka, or even just some water. Look for the "fill" line embossed on the side of the air lock and add the liquid up to that mark. Gases from the cider will bubble through the liquid as they exit the container, but the liquid will also act as a barrier to prevent things from getting in.

AUTOSIPHON An autosiphon, along with some plastic tubing (see page 28), helps you easily transfer cider from one container to another without making a big mess or disturbing the cider too much.

An autosiphon is much easier to use than its predecessor, the racking cane, and can be used just by submerging the siphon in the cider and then pumping the inner tube once or twice to start the flow of liquid. I suggest practicing a few times with regular water before attempting it with cider. Buy a shorter mini-siphon for 1-gallon batches or a full-size siphon for 5-gallon batches.

BOTTLES You can bottle your cider in any size bottle you prefer. Still (nonsparkling) ciders can be stored in wine bottles or any other container with an airtight seal. Fizzy (sparkling) cider should only be kept in bottles meant to hold pressurized and carbonated liquids, like brown 12-ounce beer bottles, 22-ounce beer bottles, or flip-top bottles. Make sure you buy these bottles from a homebrew store since bottles from other sources may not have been manufactured for bottling carbonated beverages.

It's fine to save and reuse bottles, but make sure they are thoroughly cleaned before using and discard any that show nicks or cracks around the lip. Use dark-colored bottles to protect your cider from sunlight, which can give it a stale, cardboard-like flavor.

A 1-gallon batch of cider will give you eight to ten 12-ounce bottles. A 5-gallon batch will give you forty-eight to fifty 12-ounce bottles.

BOTTLE CAPS Buy oxygen-absorbing crown caps to bottle your cider. The oxygen-absorbing material helps prevent oxidization, which can give your cider cooked, sherry-like flavors. Crown caps fit over the mouth of standard 12-ounce and 22-ounce beer bottles. Use a bottle capper to pinch the crown around the lip of the bottle and seal it tight.

Unlike beer bottles, the caps cannot be reused. Purchase new bottle caps with every batch you make.

BOTTLE CAPPER An inexpensive butterfly bottle capper works just fine for capping bottles. It looks a bit like a butterfly or a bird in flight. You place the bottle cap on the bottle, position the capper over the top, and then press gently down on the "wings." This crimps the cap around the lip of the bottle.

BOTTLE FILLER A bottle filler makes filling bottles with ciders very easy. Attach it to the open end of your siphon assembly (your autosiphon and the tubing) when you're ready to bottle. Insert it into a bottle until the spring-loaded tip presses against the bottom, and cider will start to flow. Fill until the cider reaches the lip of the bottle, then lift the bottle filler out. The flow of cider will stop immediately, preventing overflow.

PLASTIC BUCKET

AUTOSIPHON

PLASTIC TUBING

HYDROMETER

BOTTLE

BOTTLE CAPPER

GLASS JUG

AIR LOCK

WINE THIEF

BOTTLE FILLER

BOTTLE CAPS

GLASS JUG OR CARBOY AND DRILLED STOPPER

Glass jugs (1-gallon) or carboys (5-gallon) are used to hold the cider during the slower, more leisurely secondary stage of fermentation and aging. Use a 1-gallon jug for 1-gallon batches and a 5-gallon carboy for 5-gallon batches. The cozy environment reduces the amount of surface area exposed to air.

Pick up a drilled stopper for your jug or carboy, as well. You'll insert the air lock into the drilled hole and use the stopper to plug up the neck of the container. This creates a closed system, protecting the cider.

Also, although not strictly necessary, a second jug or carboy can be very helpful for making multiple batches of cider at once, or for times when you want to transfer the cider off its sediment for longer aging.

HYDROMETER AND HYDROMETER TEST JAR

Wondering how to figure out the alcohol content of your cider? A hydrometer is the tool you need. This gets a little science-y, so bear with me: A hydrometer measures the density of liquids, called their "gravity." In the case of cider, sugars in the apple juice increase its density. As the yeast eats those sugars and produce alcohol, the density drops. If you use a hydrometer to measure the density at the start of fermentation and then again at the end, you'll know how much sugar has been consumed and therefore how much alcohol has been created.

This is all much easier than it sounds. Fill the hydrometer test jar (which looks like a tall, skinny cylinder) about three-quarters full with apple juice. Drop in the hydrometer and let it float. Where the surface of the liquid intersects the hydrometer, you'll see a number, usually in the range of 1.000 to 1.150. That number is your "original gravity reading" (OG). Before fermentation, the OG of apple juice averages about 1.060; a higher number indicates higher sugar content. Record this number somewhere handy.

Take a second reading when the cider is finished (the "final gravity reading," or FG). For cider, the final gravity will usually be around 1.000. Then plug the two numbers into this formula to calculate the alcohol by volume percent (ABV):

$$(\text{FINAL GRAVITY} - \text{ORIGINAL GRAVITY}) \times 131.25 = \text{ALCOHOL BY VOLUME PERCENT}$$

If you don't really care about the alcohol content of your cider, you can skip this fuss. Without any added sugar, most homemade ciders wind up between 6 percent and 8 percent ABV.

MESH HOP BAG (6 BY 8 INCHES) This small bag is great for adding not only hops to your cider, but also small doses of any flavoring ingredient. I usually sanitize it before adding the ingredient and then knot the top closed. To make the bag easier to remove after infusing, knot a piece of unflavored floss or thin plastic twine around the bag and let the long end hang out the top of the jug or bucket so it's trapped beneath the jug stopper or bucket lid. Mesh bags can be machine or hand washed and reused.

MESH FRUIT BAG (29 BY 29 INCHES) Loose fruit or other ingredients can tend to clog up the siphon when you're trying to transfer the cider. It's much more convenient to place all the fruit in one of these large mesh bags. The bag keeps the fruit contained and makes it easy to separate from the cider. I usually sanitize the bag before adding the fruit by submerging it in sanitizer and then knot the top or cinch it closed with a sanitized rubber band. To make the bag easier to remove after infusing, knot a piece of unflavored floss or thin plastic twine around the bag and let the long end hang out the top of the jug or bucket so it's beneath the jug stopper or bucket lid. Mesh bags can be machine or hand washed and reused.

PLASTIC BUCKET AND LID I like to use a plastic bucket for the first, very active stage of fermentation. There's a lot of bubbling and fizzing that goes on in those first few days, and the extra space in the bucket means that there's plenty of room for the cider to do its thing without risk that it will bubble up—or out. A bucket is also easier to clean than a jug or carboy (your other options for this stage of fermentation), and since the first stage of fermentation leaves behind a lot of gunk and sediment, cleanability is an important consideration.

Get a 2-gallon bucket for smaller 1-gallon batches of cider and a 6.5-gallon bucket for larger 5-gallon batches. If you buy your bucket from somewhere other than a homebrew supply store (like a hardware store), just be sure that the bucket is made of food-grade white plastic. Also be sure to buy a lid with a rubber-lined hole in the top. This is where you'll insert the air lock, which allows the gases produced during fermentation to escape.

PLASTIC TUBING (5/16 INCH) AND CLAMP Along with an autosiphon, this plastic tubing is part of the siphon assembly used to transfer cider between containers. Get about 5 feet of tubing, and cut it down to a manageable length, if necessary, once you set up the siphon assembly (better too much than too little tubing). A clamp on the open end is useful for controlling or shutting off the flow of cider.

SANITIZER Though technically not equipment in the same sense as these other tools, sanitizer is still a vital part of your cider-making kit. It's extremely important to make sure all your equipment is thoroughly sanitized before it comes into contact with your apple juice or cider. This minimizes the risk of your apple juice or cider picking up an infection anywhere along the way.

There are two sanitizers I like to use, Star San and One Step, but any food-grade sanitizer will work just fine. To use most of them, you dilute a small amount of sanitizer in a specific amount of water. I often use my plastic bucket for this and throw all the equipment I need to sanitize right into the bucket. (You can also sanitize the lid by wedging it into the bucket sideways and partially submerging it in the sanitizer; rotate it a few times to be sure the entire surface is sanitized.) Check the instructions that come with your sanitizer to see how long your equipment needs to be in contact with the sanitizer and whether you need to rinse your equipment afterward.

WINE THIEF A wine thief lets you sneak little tastes out of the jug so you can gauge how the cider is progressing. It looks like a long, thick straw and is made of either glass or plastic. Glass wine thieves are very delicate, so be careful when using them.

Sanitize the thief before using, and then carefully stick one end into the cider. Wait for a moment until you see the cider partially fill the thief, then place your thumb over the top of the tube and pull out your sample. Hold the thief over a cup and lift your thumb to release the sample.

cider-making ingredients

While apple juice is certainly the star of the show when it comes to cider, a few other ingredients play supporting roles and help make sure each batch is successful. You'll find all of these ingredients at homebrew supply stores or online. With the exception of the yeast and bacteria cultures, all of them will keep for months in the cupboard, so feel free to stock up so they are handy whenever the mood strikes to make a batch of cider.

ACID BLEND One of the qualities of a really good cider is that, just ever so slightly, it makes your mouth pucker. This sweet-tart flavor typically comes from acidic apples, like Granny Smiths, but sometimes your cider needs a little help. For these times, there's powdered acid blend.

This blend is typically a mix of equal parts citric acid, malic acid, and tartaric acid. Each one of these acids has a slightly different quality, which combine to give you a rounded, balanced acidic flavor. You can buy premade blends, or mix it yourself.

I generally wait to add any acid blend until close to bottling. This way, I can see how much natural acidity is in my finished cider and add acid blend accordingly. Start with about ½ teaspoon per gallon, taste, and add more if needed. Acid blend will dissolve quickly in the cider and the change in flavor should be immediate.

MALOLACTIC BACTERIA CULTURE Apples contain a lot of malic acid. In small amounts, this adds a pleasant, bracing acidic flavor to ciders, but it can make a cider taste aggressively tart in larger amounts. Malolactic bacteria converts this malic acid into milder lactic acid, giving you a cider with a softer, more tempered acidity. In the cider-making and wine-making industries, this process is called "malolactic fermentation," or MLF.

If you use fresh-pressed juice and don't add any potassium metabisulfites, there is usually enough malolactic bacteria in the juice so that the cider will undergo this process naturally. If you use pasteurized juice or have added sulfites, then you can add commercial malolactic bacteria to kick off the conversion process.

Add the malolactic bacteria any time after the primary fermentation is complete. Give it at least a month to complete malolactic fermentation, and then bottle.

PECTIC ENZYMES Apples contain quite a bit of natural pectin. This substance is highly useful for making jams and jellies that set firmly, but not so much when we're talking about a batch of cider. Here, pectin can give ciders a hazy, cloudy appearance called "pectin haze." This doesn't alter the flavor or the texture of the cider, but it's annoying and a sign of imperfection in classic ciders.

Pectic enzymes are here to save the day! These enzymes destroy pectin, and ½ teaspoon per gallon added at the start of fermentation will help make sure your cider finishes crystal clear. (FYI, since pasteurization changes the basic structure of the juice, ciders made with pasteurized juice sometimes remain hazy, or may be very slow to clear, even when pectic enzyme is used.)

POTASSIUM METABISULFITES (CAMPDEN TABLETS) More generally referred to as "sulfites," this chemical compound acts as a preservative, stabilizer, and antioxidant in cider. When added before fermentation begins, it helps inhibit the growth of wild yeast and spoilage-causing bacteria, especially in fresh-pressed, unpasteurized juice. (Sulfites aren't needed for pasteurized juice.) Added once fermentation is complete, sulfites help stabilize the color and flavor of the cider, prevent oxidization, and give the cider a longer shelf life. Sulfites can also prevent malolactic fermentation from occurring, if that is desired.

Potassium metabisulfites are commonly sold to homebrewers in the form of Campden tablets. Use one tablet per gallon of juice or cider, and crush it into a powder with the back of a spoon or with a mortar and pestle before adding it to the liquid. Wait 24 hours for the sulfites to do their job and dissipate, and then add yeast or any other additional ingredients to the juice or cider.

Also, a heads-up: sulfites can cause an allergic reaction for some people. If you are sensitive to sulfites, or are concerned that your future drinking companions might be, then either stick to using pasteurized juice or just skip the sulfites altogether. Sulfites provide some nice insurance against spoilage, but aren't essential for a successful batch of cider.

POTASSIUM SORBATE Potassium sorbate is a food preservative that inhibits the growth of bacteria and yeast. It is only needed if you would like to sweeten your cider before bottling without risk of kick-starting another round of fermentation.

Potassium metabisulfites and potassium sorbate are a one-two punch. First, wait until the cider has completely finished fermenting and you've seen no signs of activity for a few weeks. Then add potassium metabisulfite and let it do its work for 24 hours. The next day, follow up with potassium sorbate at a rate of ½ teaspoon per gallon. If any yeast cells have survived the sulfite stage, the sorbate will make sure they don't reproduce. After another 24-hour wait, you can sweeten the cider to taste and bottle.

This method works well for preventing the refermentation of the cider in almost all cases, but it's not totally guaranteed. I've had occasional batches where a few resilient yeast cells somehow survived and got the fermentation party going again. I recommend opening a bottle about a month after bottling to check for refermentation. If all is well, the cider will be still (nonsparkling) and will taste just the same as when you bottled; if fermentation has started again, the cider will now be sparkling and significantly less sweet. If you suspect fermentation has restarted, refrigerate all bottles immediately to avoid having any of them explode and then drink within a few weeks.

PRIMING SUGAR Priming sugar is only used when you want to make a carbonated, sparkling cider and is an umbrella term referring to any fermentable sugar added for purposes of carbonation. The sugar is like a last snack for the remaining yeast; the yeast eats the extra bit of sugar and creates a tiny amount of carbon

dioxide. Since the carbon dioxide stays trapped inside the bottle, this is what makes the cider carbonated and fizzy.

Any kind of fermentable sugar will work, but for ciders, I like to use corn sugar, honey, or maple syrup. Corn sugar is available at homebrewing stores and adds fizz to ciders without giving it any extra flavor. Honey and maple syrup will add a little honey or maple flavor, respectively. This can be a nice complement to many ciders but is not always desired.

Priming sugar is always added in a very specific amount, whether you're using corn sugar, honey, or maple syrup. You want enough to carbonate the cider, but not so much that pressure builds inside the bottle and the bottle explodes. Always follow the recipe instructions and measure carefully.

WINE TANNIN Tannins add a slightly bitter, astringent, drying quality to cider, like sipping on a cup of plain black tea or a glass of dark red wine. This might not sound entirely pleasant, but tannins are actually a key component to making a well-balanced cider. You want just enough tannin so that you know it's there, but not so much that your tongue goes bone-dry when you try to swallow.

Some apples are naturally tannic, particularly cider apples, crabapples, and quince. Ciders made with a good portion of these fruits in the juice mix are good to go. But if your finished cider seems to be lacking bitterness or body, you can add both by using powdered wine tannin. (Be sure to buy wine tannin, not tannic acid or any other similar-sounding ingredient.)

This powdered tannin is soluble in liquid and can be added at any stage of fermentation. I like to add it toward the end, once I have a good idea of the finished flavors and characters in the cider. Add a small dose of ⅛ to ½ teaspoon per gallon, and gently swirl it into the cider. You'll notice a flavor difference right away, but it's good to wait a few days and taste it again before adding another dose. Add more if needed, but be cautious since it's easy to overdo it.

YEAST Aside from the juice itself, yeast is the one other ingredient that's absolutely essential for making cider. It's a living, breathing organism, and it's the job of the yeast to convert the sugars in the apple juice into alcohol and carbon dioxide. No yeast, no cider!

Fresh, unpasteurized apple juice actually contains a nice population of natural yeast already. This "wild" yeast is more than adequate for fermenting juice into cider, and this is how cider was made for centuries. Wild yeast takes longer to complete fermentation than commercial yeast, but it can also make a cider with outstanding complexity and character. Since this yeast will be totally unique to the apples it came from and the orchard where those apples were grown, you will literally be making a cider like none other.

You also have a vast array of commercial yeast available to you, from wine yeast and beer yeast to those specifically designed for fermenting cider. Each yeast strain has its own particular character, which imprints itself on the taste and flavor of your cider and gives you endless options and variations in the ciders you make. Beer yeast tends to make ciders with a rustic, somewhat spicy quality. Wine yeast gives ciders a more refined character with mellow fruit flavors. Champagne yeast, in particular, makes a very dry cider. As you try different yeast, you will likely find yourself gravitating toward one in particular. Everyone's tastes and preferences are a little different!

In developing the recipes for this book, I primarily used the following yeast varieties.

- **Brettanomyces yeast:** White labs WLP650 Brettanomyces Bruxellensis (liquid yeast)
- **English ale yeast:** Safale S-04 and Danstar Nottingham Dry Ale Yeast
- **Cider yeast:** Safcider and White Labs WLP775 English Cider (liquid yeast)
- **California ale yeast:** Safale US-05
- **Belgian ale yeast:** Safbrew S-33 and Safbrew T-58
- **Lager yeast:** Saflager S-23
- **Wheat beer yeast:** Safbrew WB-06
- **White wine yeast:** Red Star Montrachet Dry Wine Yeast and Red Star Côte des Blancs Dry Wine Yeast
- **Red wine yeast:** Red Star Pasteur Red Dry Wine Yeast
- **Champagne yeast:** Red Star Pasteur Champagne Dry Yeast

Use half a package of either dry or liquid yeast for a 1-gallon batch and a full package for a 5-gallon batch. Technically, half a package is more than you need for a 1-gallon batch, but measuring smaller amounts starts to feel overly fussy and the extra yeast doesn't do any harm. The leftover yeast from making a 1-gallon batch can be saved for another batch of cider. It will keep for a few months in an airtight container in the fridge.

One very important thing to consider: If you are gluten-free or if you might be serving your cider to friends who are gluten-free, double check that the yeast you use is also gluten-free. Most varieties of dry yeast are gluten-free; liquid yeasts are often cultured on a malt grain base and are not gluten-free.

YEAST NUTRIENTS For all its other great qualities, apple juice is lacking in many of the proper nutrients needed for a strong, healthy fermentation. The yeast will still ferment the juice without these nutrients, but they're a lot happier if they have them and happy yeast mean better cider.

Most homebrewing stores sell yeast nutrients as powdered blends, which contain a mix of vitamins, minerals, and other compounds that help ensure strong fermentation. Check the package instructions for how much to add to your batch, since this differs from brand to brand. Add yeast nutrients along with the yeast itself at the start of fermentation.

cider-flavoring ingredients

A classic cider made strictly from apple juice is all fine and dandy, but we're *modern* cider makers, aren't we? We occasionally like to go off-script and experiment with other flavor combinations in our ciders. Here are a few of my favorites, which you'll find in many of the recipes in this book.

Just a heads-up: many sweet ingredients, like fruit, fruit juice, or honey, will add extra fermentable sugars to your cider along with the flavor boost. This will increase the alcohol content in your finished cider.

DRIED FRUIT I like using dried fruit when I just want a subtle fruitiness in my ciders. Their flavor tends to be more mellow than fresh fruit or fruit juice. Dried fruit can also add some unfermentable sugars to your cider, which means that some sugar is left behind even after fermentation is complete. This gives you a cider that tastes slightly sweeter and more full-bodied without the need for fussy back-sweetening methods (see page 52).

Start with a cup of dried fruit per gallon and add more in the following weeks if you find you want a stronger flavor. Coarsely chop any larger fruit, like figs or apricots, and place all fruit in a small mesh hop bag or a larger fruit bag (see page 27) to help make it easier to add to and remove the fruit from the cider.

Add the dried fruit to the cider once active fermentation slows, at which point the alcohol in the cider will help protect it from any bacteria you might introduce with the fruit.

FRESH FRUIT Sometimes I like to throw the whole dang fruit into the mix, not just the juice. The skin, the flesh of the fruit, and even the seeds can all add interesting flavors and aromas to the cider. The amount of fruit you need depends on the fruit itself and how much of its flavor you want in your cider. Start with a cup or two per gallon and add more if you end up wanting a stronger flavor.

Make sure to wash fresh fruit thoroughly and rinse away any soap or cleaners. If the fruit is large, like a peach or plum, chop it up into small pieces. Remove any pits, stems, or other bits, but I usually leave the skins on. Put the fruit into a mesh fruit bag (see page 27) to make it easier to add and remove from the fermentation container. Crush fruit lightly in a bowl or other container before adding it and its juice to the cider. Crushing releases some of the fruit juice and breaks open the cell structure of the fruit to make it easier to infuse into the cider.

Add the fruit and any collected juice to the cider once active fermentation has slowed, but before you transfer it to the jug or carboy (where there's less room for larger volumes of extra ingredients). At this point, there is enough alcohol in the cider to protect it from most spoilage-causing bacteria. The alcohol also helps pull the flavor of the fruit into the cider, giving you a brighter, cleaner fruit flavor. Infuse for at least a week, or up to a month.

Frozen fruit is also a great choice for making cider, especially if you get a hankering for a fruity cider in the middle of the winter or any other time fresh fruit is hard to find. Let the frozen fruit thaw in the fridge overnight before adding it to cider. I also recommend using a mesh bag when working with frozen fruit.

FRUIT JUICE The same guidelines for apple juice quality apply to any other fruit juices you may want to use in your cider-making adventures, like cherry, pomegranate, or pineapple juice. The juice you press yourself or buy directly from the farm usually makes the best cider, but juice from the grocery store is still a fine choice. Buy the best-quality and freshest juice you can find and afford.

HONEY, MAPLE SYRUP, AND OTHER SUGARS You get two things when you add honey, maple syrup, or any other sugary sweetener to your cider. First, you add a little extra flavor to your cider. Second, you increase the alcohol content. These are fermentable sugars, meaning that yeast is able to ferment them into alcohol, so any extra sugar you add becomes more food for the yeast.

This extra flavor isn't "sweet," per se. It's more like the essence of whatever sweetener you've added. Honey has its own particular honey flavor, maple syrup has its own unique maple-y flavor, and so on. Only pure white sugar doesn't really have a flavor of its own; use it when you want to boost the alcohol of your cider without affecting its overall flavor.

I love experimenting with syrups and sweeteners in my ciders! Buckwheat honey has become a favorite while working on the recipes for this book; even in small doses, this dark honey adds a really beautiful nutty, caramel flavor to ciders. Molasses also adds an intriguing flavor that reminds me of slightly smoky

burnt sugar. It's become impossible to walk down the baking aisle at the grocery store or past the honey vendor the farmers' market without picking up something new to try.

HOPS Hops are fragrant light-green flowers that look (somewhat confusingly) like tiny pinecones. They're primarily used when making beer, but they are darn good in a batch of cider as well.

You'll find hops at homebrew stores and online. You'll sometimes find the whole, fresh hop flower, but more often, they are sold as compressed pellets. Either works fine for our purposes.

There are dozens of different hop varieties to choose from. Some hops smell like tropical fruit, others add earthy and spicy flavors, while still others have an aroma like walking through a pine forest. All the flavors are natural, not artificial. For this, you can thank the pure botanical magic of the hop flower.

The best way to add hops to cider is a method called "dry hopping." Just wait until the first active stage of fermentation has slowed, then add your dose of hops. Start with a small amount, like a teaspoon or two per gallon, and add more if you end up wanting a stronger aroma or flavor. Enclosing them in a small mesh hop bag (see page 27) helps make them easier to add and remove, and also prevents the hop sediment from clogging your siphon when you bottle. However, don't worry if some of the dissolved hops work their way through the bag and fall into the cider; this will eventually settle to the bottom of your jug or carboy and shouldn't change the flavor too much.

For even more hop flavor, boil some hops with half of your juice before fermentation. Don't boil for longer than 15 minutes, however, or you'll reduce the cider by too much and develop cooked flavors in your cider.

For you beer brewers out there who might be thinking of doing a hop boil with your cider, my recommendation is to let that dream go. A full hour-long boil concentrates the cider and gives it a strange cooked flavor, like sad applesauce. Cider also doesn't seem to extract the bittering component from the hops in quite the same way as beer, which renders the whole endeavor rather pointless. However, if you do your own experiments and find success, please let me know!

OAK CUBES Oak cubes are your ticket to making a "barrel-aged" cider without investing in an actual barrel. These tiny little cubes of charred oak come in a range of different "toast" levels, from light to dark; I usually use cubes with a medium toast level for cider. Look for them at homebrew supply stores and online.

The best way to use oak cubes is to soak them in a flavorful liquor, like bourbon or rum, and then add them (and sometimes the liquor used for soaking) directly to the cider once active fermentation is complete. You don't need much to give your cider a subtle boozy, oaky flavor. A ½ ounce of cubes soaked in a few ounces of liquor per gallon of cider will get the job done. Putting the cubes in a small mesh hop bag (see page 27) makes them easy to add and remove.

Taste your barrel-aged cider weekly while it's mingling with the oak cubes. The flavor can go from pleasantly oaky to tasting like wet pencil shavings very quickly. As soon as the cider reaches a flavor you like, bottle the cider or pull out the oak cubes. If the woody taste becomes too strong, add some fresh apple juice to the jug to dilute the cider (the cider will start to ferment again, so wait to bottle).

OTHER PANTRY INGREDIENTS The whole of your pantry is open to you for your cider-making experiments. Dried whole spices, vanilla beans, flaked coconut, cacao nibs, even dried chile peppers—all of these sweet and savory ingredients are ready, willing, and able to contribute their flavors to your cider. (Don't use powdered or ground spices; they can overinfuse your cider and make it taste bitter.)

There are only three rules here. First, make sure the ingredients you use are fresh. The best way to judge this is by opening up the bag or container and taking a sniff. If an ingredient is fresh, it will still have a very strong and pleasant aroma. If it's past its prime, the fragrance will be very faint or gone altogether. If you're not sure, err on the side of caution and pick up some fresh ingredients. Musty spices and desiccated old vanilla beans are not likely to do much for your cider, and might even add some unwelcome flavors.

Second, add ingredients in small doses. A little will go a long way, especially with dried spices. More spice flavor isn't always as straightforward as doubling or tripling the amount you add, which is why I sometimes use different ratios of spices in my 1-gallon batches than in my 5-gallon batches. My philosophy is that you can always add more, but you can't take it out once it's there. Let the smaller amount infuse for a week or so, then taste your cider and add more if you'd like a stronger flavor. Use mesh bags (see page 27) to make the spices easy to add and remove.

Third, and finally, remove the ingredients once they have infused to your liking. Many pantry ingredients will continue to infuse and become stronger the longer they sit, and what was once a perfect smattering of spicy goodness will slowly become as bitter as a cough drop with time. If the flavor becomes too strong, you can always mix in extra apple juice to dilute the cider, but avoidance is really the better strategy.

To make the bag of ingredients easier to remove, knot a piece of unflavored floss or thin plastic twine around the bag and let the long end hang out the top of the jug or bucket. Seal the jug or bucket as normal, trapping the floss beneath the jug stopper or bucket lid (unless your floss or twine is very thick, the jug or bucket will still create a tight seal). Once the cider is infused, pull out the bag using the floss. Alternatively, you can use any tool with a hook to remove the bag, bottle the cider immediately, or siphon the cider to a fresh jug or carboy to separate it from the ingredients.

turning juice into cider

At its heart, making cider is really very simple. I think it's all too easy to get caught up in the shiny new equipment, the quest for perfect apples, and the unfamiliar processes, and forget that fact. For centuries, cider is how people made good use of an abundance of fruit and also ensured they had something safe and tasty to drink with their meals. There's nothing particularly tricky or mysterious about how cider is made. Apple juice *wants* to become cider. Your main job as a cider maker is really to just guide things along the tastiest path possible.

All cider, traditional and modern, is made in basically the same way. You put the cider in a closed container, and either introduce some yeast or let the natural yeast take over. Then you leave it alone.

The yeast goes to work right away consuming all the sugar in the apple juice, and in the process, it produces carbon dioxide and alcohol. The carbon dioxide mostly bubbles up and out of the fermentation container, but the alcohol stays put. It's the presence of alcohol that means our batch of fermenting apple juice is now an honest-to-goodness cider.

The first week or two of fermentation is the most active, but as the sugars become scarce, the yeast party slows and gradually comes to an end. The inactive yeast settles to the bottom of the jug along with various other solid particles, leaving the cider clear and still. The cider is then bottled, and in fairly short order, it's ready to drink. At an average room temperature of about 70°F, this whole process will usually happen in about a month.

When I say all cider is made this way, I really do mean *all* of it. The scale may be different and some details may change, but this basic progression from juice to cider is the same for commercial cider makers and for those of us at home. Perhaps even more amazing, the process was exactly the same for cider makers hundreds of years ago as it is today.

how to make cider

Think of the following steps as your cider-making trail guide. We'll go over all the ins and outs of the process, from when to add the yeast to bottling your finished cider. Every batch of cider you make will use the same basic procedures, so it's good to spend some time here learning how everything is done. Later, if you get lost or have questions while you're making one of the ciders in the book, come back here to get reoriented.

STEP 1 // clean and sanitize your equipment

Sanitation is important. As cider makers, we want to create an environment where the only organisms interacting with our juice or our cider are the ones we invite there. This means that any equipment that comes into contact with the juice or cider at any stage of the game needs to be thoroughly cleaned and sanitized.

First, wash everything with soap and water. Rinse thoroughly so that you're sure no detergent remains. Fill your plastic fermentation bucket with sanitizer and submerge everything inside—tubes, the air lock, the lid, a whisk, and all other equipment you need at this point. Check the instructions that came with your sanitizer for information on how long the equipment needs to stay submerged and if it needs to be rinsed after sanitizing. Once sanitized, the equipment can be laid out on clean kitchen towels until needed. Before emptying the fermentation bucket, pour a little sanitizer into a mixing bowl just in case you have a last-minute sanitizing emergency. (When sanitizing the equipment needed for transferring or bottling your cider in the later stages of cider making, you can use a large mixing bowl, a clean plastic bin, or any other large container if your fermenter is in use.)

Sanitation is particularly important at the beginning of fermentation. This is when the juice is most vulnerable and can easily spoil or pick up an infection if equipment isn't thoroughly sanitized. Once fermentation is solidly underway and the cider has developed some alcohol, it does a pretty good job of keeping itself protected. Even so, it's better to be safe than sorry. Repeat the sanitizing step at every stage of the cider-making process, bucket to bottle.

STEP 2 // start your cider

Pour all the apple juice into a sanitized fermentation bucket. It's fine if the juice is still cold from the fridge, but make sure it's thawed if it was frozen. Use a 2-gallon bucket for a 1-gallon batch of cider or a 6.5-gallon bucket for a 5-gallon batch. The extra space in the bucket gives the juice some room to bubble and foam during the first active stage of fermentation without risk that it will push the lid off.

CHECK THE ORIGINAL GRAVITY

At this point, before any fermentation has started, it's good practice to check and record the original gravity, or OG, of your juice using a hydrometer. This device measures the density of the liquid, and since the density of juice is primarily influenced by its sugar content, this means you can get a reasonable idea of how much sugar is in your juice. As fermentation progresses and sugar is converted into alcohol by the yeast, the density of the liquid will drop. If you take a second reading (the final gravity, or FG) after fermentation is complete, you can compare the two numbers and use them to determine the final alcohol by volume (ABV) of the cider (see page 27).

To take a gravity reading, first sanitize both the hydrometer and the hydrometer test jar. Then fill the test jar about three-quarters full with juice and insert the hydrometer. The hydrometer will float in the liquid (if not, add more juice until it does). Look at where the surface of the juice bisects the hydrometer and record that number, which should be between 1.000 and 1.150. On average, with no extra sugar added, most apple juice will typically have an OG of around 1.060. Record the number somewhere handy and return the juice to the bucket.

TREAT UNPASTEURIZED APPLE JUICE WITH SULFITES (IF YOU WANT)

If you are using pasteurized juice to make your cider, there's no need to do anything more. You can skip this section entirely!

Raw, unpasteurized juice does not need to be pasteurized or otherwise sterilized before being used to make cider (see "Pasteurization and Apple Juice," page 19). However, in recipes that call for commercial yeast, I recommend treating the raw juice with Campden tablets (potassium metabisulfite) to minimize competition from the wild yeast present in the juice. These sulfites won't affect the flavor or character of the finished cider, and they dissipate within 24 hours.

Note that sulfites can cause a mild allergic reaction with a small percentage of people. If you or anyone in your family is sensitive to sulfites, you can skip using them with minimal risk to your cider. Sulfites are like an insurance policy: you can often get by just fine without them, but they minimize risk and help you sleep better at night. (By the way, most wine is also treated with sulfites; if you can drink wine without a reaction, then you'll be okay with sulfites in your cider.)

The role of sulfites is to neutralize the spoilage-causing bacteria in the juice as well as most of the wild yeast. This reduces the risk of infection and also clears the way for the commercial yeast. Using them means a clean fermentation without the risk that some wild yeast might step in and muddy things up. Skip them whenever you want to encourage, rather than supress, a wild yeast fermentation in the cider.

If you've decided to add sulfites, here's what you do: crush one Campden tablet per gallon of juice with a spoon or a mortar and pestle, and whisk into the juice with a sanitized whisk. Attach the sanitized lid and an air lock filled with a little sanitizer or vodka. Wait a full 24 hours for the sulfites to do their job and dissipate. If you add yeast before the sulfites have dissipated, your fermentation might get off to a sluggish start since the sulfites will interfere with the yeast. Also, don't wait for too long after the 24 hours are up before adding the yeast or the cider might start to spoil despite adding sulfites.

ADD THE YEAST

When you're ready to continue, sprinkle the yeast, yeast nutrient, and pectic enzyme over the surface of the juice. Whisk the juice with a sanitized whisk until it's foamy in order to dissolve the ingredients and add some air into the juice. This is the only time in the whole cider-making process where some extra oxygen is actually desirable. Here, it helps ensure a fast and strong start to fermentation (the yeast needs some oxygen to help it reproduce in the initial stages); at any other time, too much oxygen can oxidize the cider and give it some stale sherry-like flavors or turn it into vinegar.

Snap on the sanitized lid, making sure it creates a tight seal all the way around the bucket. Fill the air lock with sanitizer or vodka and insert it into the lid. Place the bucket of juice somewhere out of the way and out of direct sunlight at a steady temperature of 70° to 75°F.

STEP 3 // start primary fermentation

Fermentation should begin within one to two days at room temperature. During this lag time, the yeast is primarily working on growing its population and getting situated before charging full tilt into active fermentation. Resist the urge to open the bucket and check on your cider during this time. This is a very vulnerable period for the cider and you could easily introduce an infection by accident.

You'll know fermentation has started when you see bubbles popping up through the liquid in the air lock. You may just see one or two bubbles at first, but once fermentation gets going, you'll see a steady stream burbling through the air lock. If you put your ear to the bucket, you'll also hear a steady fizzing noise, like an open bottle of soda. This is the sound of the yeast at work! It's eating its way through the sugars in the juice and releasing tiny bubbles of carbon dioxide in the process.

You might notice a gassy, fruity aroma in the area around your bucket, particularly if you're storing it in an enclosed space. If it bothers you, move the cider to a spot with better airflow; the aroma will dissipate once active fermentation slows. Again, resist the urge

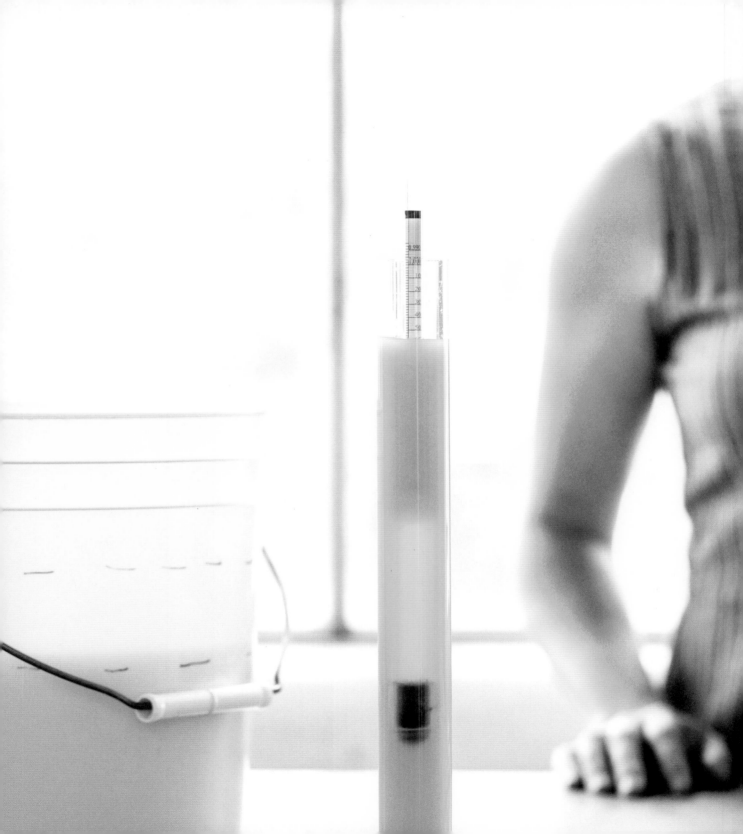

to open the lid and check on your cider during this time. As long as you are seeing bubbles in the air lock, trust that fermentation is proceeding normally.

FERMENTATION TEMPERATURE

Pay attention to the temperature in the place where you are storing the cider during this time, since it affects fermentation. Warmer temperatures make the yeast work faster and speed up fermentation, while cooler temperatures slow everything down. The sweet spot for most yeast is between 65° and 75°F—this is where they are happiest and do their best fermentation work. However, they are generally fine within a larger range of 50° to 85°F. Below 50°F, the yeast starts to get sleepy and slow, and it might stop fermenting altogether. Above 85°F, the yeast literally gets stressed out, and you will start to notice a lot of unpleasantly yeasty and harsh alcohol-like flavors in the cider. (See Troubleshooting Your Homemade Cider, page 169, for what to do during heat waves and cold spells.)

By the way, there are some real advantages to fermenting your cider a little cooler, if you can. Between 55° and 60°F, fermentation proceeds at a steady, controlled pace rather than the all-out feeding frenzy of warmer temperatures. The slow fermentation means that the cider develops a more nuanced character with delicate aromas and flavors. The process takes a little longer, but the end result is a more sophisticated cider. A temperature-controlled fridge is great for this slow fermentation, but you might also try your basement or the corner in an unheated entryway during the winter months.

This primary stage of fermentation only lasts for a week or two, or a little longer if fermentation temperatures are cool. Keep a close watch on the air lock. You'll notice the bubbling peak within a few days after the start of fermentation and then gradually start to slow. You might still see a stray bubble or two in the air lock, but most of the fermentation will finish within about two weeks.

STEP 4 // transfer the cider to the jug or carboy

Once fermentation slows and you've seen very little, or no, activity in the air lock for a few days, you can transfer your cider from the fermentation bucket to a smaller, cozier jug or carboy. Transfer to a 1-gallon glass jug for 1-gallon batches or a 5-gallon glass carboy for 5-gallon batches.

There are a few reasons for doing this. The main one is simple housekeeping. A lot of solid particles sink to the bottom of the cider once fermentation slows, and it's good practice to separate your lovely cider from this leftover sludge as soon as you have a chance. This sludge of used-up yeast, apple solids, proteins, and other materials can start to give your cider some swampy, stagnant flavors from decomposition if left together for too long (more than a month or two). Also, if you go straight from bucket to bottle, you often end up transferring a lot of that sediment into the bottles, which can decrease the cider's shelf life and cause haziness in the glass.

Cider is also very susceptible to oxidation. Brief exposure to air and oxygen usually isn't a big deal, but exposure over a long period of time will eventually create flavors like stale cooking sherry or wet cardboard in your cider, or even cause it to turn into vinegar. The plastic of your fermentation bucket and the seal on the lid aren't totally impervious to oxygen; this is fine when fermentation is active and there's a lot of carbon dioxide pushing out of the bucket, but it's best to transfer the cider into a smaller glass container once that slows.

If you forget to transfer your cider or prefer to skip the hassle of moving it to a new container, just be sure to bottle your cider within a month or two to avoid picking up any unwelcome flavors.

HOW TO SIPHON YOUR CIDER

So that's *why* it's best to transfer cider to a second container. As for *how* we transfer it, we use a process called "siphoning." This uses an autosiphon, a length of tubing, and the power of gravity to smoothly suction the cider from one container into the next. Siphoning is a little trickier than just pouring the cider into its new home, but pouring would churn up a lot of the sediment we're hoping to leave behind and also splash a lot of undesired oxygen into the cider. Therefore, we siphon.

This whole siphoning process can feel rather intimidating and awkward at first. To get a feel for the process, practice a few times with plain water before you try it with a full batch of cider. You'll soon be siphoning like a pro.

Place the bucket with the cider on your kitchen counter or another counter-height surface. Place the sanitized jug or carboy on the floor, a chair, or at least a foot or so below the bucket. Sanitize your autosiphon and tubing and run some sanitizer through the inside of the equipment as well. Push a hose clamp on one end of the tubing and the other end over the shorter, crooked part of the autosiphon. Lastly, remove the lid from the bucket of cider.

Slip the autosiphon down the inside of the bucket until it hits the bottom. Try to disturb the sediment at the bottom of the bucket as little as possible. Slip the other, open end of the tubing inside the neck of the jug or carboy below.

Okay, ready? Now it's time to start siphoning! Hold the autosiphon in place against the side of the bucket with one hand. With your other hand, carefully pump the inner tube of the autosiphon once or twice. Make sure the open end of the tube stays inside the jug below while you pump. Pumping the autosiphon will create suction, pulling the cider through the autosiphon, into the tubing, and down to the jug or carboy.

Once the siphon has started, it will continue on its own until all the cider has been transferred. Keep holding the autosiphon against the side of the bucket to avoid churning up any sediment in the bucket, and keep an eye on the jug to make sure the tubing doesn't slip out. The cap on the tip of the autosiphon will prevent it from suctioning too much sediment, and the action of siphoning also creates a sediment-free pocket around the tip of the autosiphon. This said, it's okay if a little sediment gets sucked up into the siphon; it will quickly settle to the bottom of the jug or carboy in the next few days and won't adversely affect the cider. If at any

point you need to pause the siphoning, just clamp the tubing closed with a hose clamp. Also, if the flow of liquid through the siphon keeps slowing or stopping, try moving your jug a little lower.

Once almost all the cider has been transferred, gently tilt the bucket toward you to continue transferring as much of the cider as you can. You'll pull a little sediment into the siphon as you do this, but it's okay since the majority is left behind. Once the siphon becomes opaque with sediment or runs out of liquid to transfer, you're done.

TASTE YOUR CIDER AS YOU TRANSFER

While you're transferring the cider, give it a taste! This is a good moment to check on your cider and see how it's coming along. Siphon a little cider into a glass as you're transferring, or use a wine thief to draw a sample once you've finished. At this point, most of the sugars will be gone, so the cider will probably taste quite dry. It might have some sharp, overly acidic notes and some yeasty flavors. It should taste recognizable as cider, but don't worry if it doesn't seem entirely drinkable quite yet. It still has a little way to go before being done.

TOP OFF THE JUG OR CARBOY WITH JUICE, IF NEEDED

The cider should fill up the jug or carboy at least to where it starts to slope toward the neck. If you lost a lot of cider during the transferring process or if the jug doesn't seem quite full after you finish transferring, top it off with some extra apple juice to make up the loss and minimize the amount of air inside the jug or carboy. This extra juice will ferment slowly over the next few weeks and won't change the overall recipe.

Once you're done with everything, seal up the jug or carboy with a sanitized stopper and insert the filled air lock into the stopper. Stash the cider somewhere out of the way, out of direct sunlight, and at a steady temperature. Most ciders are fine fermenting at room temperature; if a different fermentation temperature is recommended, it will be specified in the recipe.

STEP 5 // age and clear the cider

Let your cider hang out for at least another two weeks before moving on to the bottling stage, or you can let it continue to age and mellow for several months. If you're aging for longer than a few weeks, make sure to top off the liquid in the air lock every so often so that the cider stays protected. It's also good to occasionally transfer the cider into a fresh jug or carboy if you see sediment starting to collect on the bottom.

This secondary phase of cider making might not look like much from the outside, but it's actually very important for making a good cider. The last bits of sugar are being discovered and broken down by the remaining active yeast. Chemicals and flavor compounds created during fermentation are also undergoing some changes. A lot of those harsh flavors you tasted when transferring the cider start to mellow out. Any remaining solid particles gradually settle to the bottom of the jug, leaving the cider itself crystal clear—though note that some ciders made with pasteurized juice may never become totally clear.

MALOLACTIC FERMENTATION

One other important process often happens during this time, and it's called malolactic fermentation (MLF). Malic acids are present to a greater or lesser degree in all apples (especially acidic apples), and these acids are responsible for the tart flavors in finished cider. Some tartness is good, but too much can throw off the balance of the cider. Through MLF, malolactic bacteria will convert the super-tart malic acid into lactic acid, which has a softer and mellower flavor.

Unpasteurized cider usually contains enough natural malolactic bacteria that it will undergo malolactic fermentation on its own at some point after yeast fermentation is complete. If you're using pasteurized juice or you used sulfites on your juice before starting, you can add commercial malolactic cultures to kick off the process. Add it any time during this secondary stage and allow 4 to 8 weeks for it to finish. (If you bottle before MLF is complete, you'll get a little extra fizz in your cider, but it shouldn't be so much as to throw off your priming sugar amounts.)

Malolactic fermentation is almost universally desirable in creating a balanced cider without sharply acidic flavors. However, if you like the flavor as it is and you'd prefer that your cider *not* go through MLF, just add a second dose of potassium metabisulfites (Campden tablets) once the cider has reached the flavor you like. The sulfites will effectively stop any further activity in the cider and preserve the flavor as it is.

TASTE YOUR CIDER AS IT AGES

Every so often during this secondary phase of aging and clearing, taste the cider using a wine thief. You'll notice that the flavors start off spiky and harsh, but then gradually smooth over time. You should also begin to taste more apple flavors coming back to the forefront. Overall, the cider should settle into itself during this period and become something you look forward to drinking.

HOW LONG TO AGE YOUR CIDER

Two weeks for this stage is the minimum. If you've been keeping your cider around 70°F and the recipe you're following didn't instruct you to add any extra sugar at the start, then by this point, fermentation should technically be complete—meaning that it's safe to bottle your cider without risk that it will continue fermenting in the bottle. If you've been fermenting your cider at cooler temperatures or if the recipe uses additional sugar, it might take a bit longer than two weeks to be sure fermentation has finished. Cider bottled while still fermenting can allow too much pressure to build up inside the bottle and potentially lead to bursting bottles.

Once fermentation is complete, you should no longer see any signs of bubbles in the air lock. You'll also notice the cider become perceptibly lighter and clearer. To make certain that fermentation is really done, you can check the specific gravity with your hydrometer. Most ciders finish with a specific gravity around 1.000; once the gravity reading holds steady for a few weeks in a row, you can safely assume fermentation is complete.

CIDER LESSON 4
getting to know acidity

GOAL
To recognize and understand the role of acidity in cider.

WHAT YOU NEED
Mass-market bottled apple juice from the pantry aisle, powdered acid blend.

WHAT TO DO
Set out six clear tumblers and pour 1 cup of juice into each one. Leave the first cup of juice plain. Add a pinch of acid blend to the second cup, 1/8 teaspoon of acid blend to the third, 1/4 teaspoon to the fourth, 1/2 teaspoon to the fifth, and 1 teaspoon to the sixth. Stir with a fork or a whisk to dissolve.

Taste each cup of juice, starting with the plain juice. The first cup will probably taste fairly sweet with very little perceptible acidity, and the last cup should taste overwhelmingly tart. Notice how the balance gradually shifts from sweet to tart, and how even just a little acidity makes the mass-market juice more interesting to drink. You don't need much, do you?

Also, notice where in the lineup you start to feel like the juice or cider becomes too tart for your taste—this is the flavor to remember and to use as a comparison when you're adjusting a batch of cider.

EXTRA CREDIT
Repeat a version of this experiment the next time you need to adjust a batch of cider. Pour about 1 cup of cider into a glass and add acid blend, one pinch at a time, until it tastes as tart as you like. Keep track of the number of pinches you add and use that number to calculate how much acid blend you need to add to the whole batch.

CIDER LESSON 5
getting to know tannins

GOAL

To recognize and understand the role of tannins in cider.

WHAT YOU NEED

Mass-market bottled apple juice from the pantry aisle, powdered wine tannin.

WHAT TO DO

Set out six clear tumblers and pour 1 cup of juice into each one. Leave the first cup of juice plain. Add 1 pinch of powdered wine tannin to the second cup, 2 pinches to the third cup, 3 pinches to the fourth, ⅛ teaspoon to the fifth, and ¼ teaspoon to the sixth. Stir with a fork or a whisk to dissolve and let stand for a few minutes before tasting.

Taste each cup of juice, starting with the plain juice. The first cup should taste like regular apple juice and the last cup should taste so woody, dry, and tannic that you can barely sip it. Somewhere in the middle, you'll notice a cup of juice that still tastes sweet, but that has a pleasant touch of woodsy bitterness in the background and that leaves a hint of dryness your mouth after you swallow. This is the kind of tannin level that you're aiming for in your ciders.

Also, look for these same bitter, drying qualities the next time you have a cup of black tea or a glass of wine. Recognizing the tannins in these beverages will help you recognize them in your cider.

EXTRA CREDIT

Repeat a version of this experiment the next time you need to adjust a batch of cider. Pour about 1 cup of cider into a glass and add powdered wine tannin, one pinch at a time, until it tastes as dry as you like. Keep track of the number of pinches you add and use that number to calculate how much tannin you need to add to the whole batch.

Letting your cider age a little longer is also never a bad thing. It will continue aging well for several months. Keep tasting it and make adjustments as needed, and then bottle when you're satisfied with the finished result. Your cider will also continue to age in the bottle, but you won't be able to taste it or make any additional adjustments.

STEP 6 // make final adjustments and back-sweeten your cider

Once you've decided you're ready to bottle the cider, it's time to think about making some final adjustments to its flavor and character. I like to wait to do this until the very end so that I have a good idea of how the finished cider tastes on its own before I start making any tweaks. If done any earlier, it's possible to misjudge the flavor or overcompensate for something that would have worked itself out later on.

These adjustments are where your personal taste—and your skill—as a cider maker really come into play, and you'll get better at it the more you do it. Think of it this way: if your cider was made with a perfect blend of sweet, acidic, and bitter apples, it should emerge tasting balanced, robust, and pleasingly complex, needing zero adjustments. More often, you'll get to this stage and feel like the cider is close, maybe even pretty good, but missing a little something.

That "something" is usually acidity, bitterness, sweetness, or some combination of the three. There are ways to adjust a cider that needs help with any of these three areas.

ADJUSTING THE ACIDITY

Let's start with adjusting the acidity. The easiest way to give your cider a perky dose of acid is by adding some powdered acid blend. This is a mix of citric acid, malic acid, and tartaric acid, and it gives cider a balanced tart flavor that hits all the right points on your tongue. You'll know your cider needs some if it tastes bland, one-dimensional, or even a little watery. Start with adding just ½ teaspoon per gallon of cider. Gently swirl it in (don't stir or overly agitate the cider), let it dissolve overnight, then give your cider another taste and add more if needed.

ADJUSTING THE TANNINS

Next, let's talk about tannins. The presence of tannins is more subtle than acids in a cider, so it can be difficult to know when you need to add some. Take a sip of your cider and pay attention to how it both tastes and feels as you hold it on your tongue and swallow. A cider with a good amount of tannins will have a touch of bitterness and leave your mouth feeling slightly dry for a second or two after you swallow. It will also have a little body; it shouldn't seem watery.

If your cider lacks this, add ⅛ teaspoon of powdered wine tannins per gallon. Swirl them in (don't stir or overly agitate the cider) and wait a few days for the flavor to fully absorb, and then taste again, continuing to adjust as needed. Too much tannin can make your cider taste like biting into a tea bag, so be careful of adding too much too quickly.

ADJUSTING THE SWEETNESS

And finally, let's discuss sweetness in your cider. First of all, know that most ciders finish very dry. In this context, "dry" just means that no more sugar remains in the cider (as opposed to the kind of "dry" that is caused by tannins). Sipping your homemade cider, you might notice some flavors that your brain still perceives as "sweet tasting," like apple flavors or honey flavors, but overall, it will taste the exact opposite.

This isn't necessarily a bad thing. Most of us have been drinking overly sweet ciders for so long that this is what we expect all ciders to taste like. In fact, a dry cider can be really beautiful. Sugary sweetness can mask subtle characteristics of the apples used to make the cider, or make a cider feel heavy and syrupy instead of light and effervescent. Your taste buds might need some time to adjust, but I encourage you to resist the urge to automatically sweeten all your ciders. Take some time to train your palate to new flavors.

All this said, a touch of sweetness in a cider is often very welcome, especially if your cider has ended up with a lot of acidity and tart flavors. In the cider-making world, sweetening a cider once fermentation is complete is called "back-sweetening." Remember that any fermentable sugar added directly to the cider will just become yeast food and result in renewed fermentation. There are several ways to sweeten your cider without this happening.

BACK-SWEETENING IN THE GLASS

The absolute easiest way to sweeten your cider (and my personal favorite) is wait to add any sweetener at all. Instead, add it directly to the glass when you're ready to serve. Make a simple syrup by simmering equal parts sugar and water until the sugar is dissolved, and then add a tablespoon or two to each glass to sweeten the cider as much as you like. You can also use honey, maple syrup, or any other kind of sweetener in place of the sugar. The simple syrup will keep for several weeks in the fridge.

BACK-SWEETENING USING UNFERMENTABLE SUGARS

Second best is to sweeten the cider with an unfermentable sugar like Splenda, Equal, or stevia. Yeast isn't interested in unfermentable sugars (hence their designation as "unfermentable"), so you can add as much as you like. Start with a little, give it a taste, and then add more until you're happy with the flavor.

BACK-SWEETENING AFTER USING SULFITES AND POTASSIUM SORBATE

Things get trickier if you'd rather stick to natural sugars since these are almost all fermentable. Your best and easiest option here is to neutralize all remaining yeast and bacteria in the cider using a combination of potassium metabisulfites and potassium sorbate. *Do not use this method if your cider underwent malolactic fermentation; adding potassium sorbate can give the cider a geranium-like aroma.*

First, wait until you're sure that fermentation is complete and the cider has become clear, which means the majority of the remaining yeast has fallen to the bottom. If you can, transfer the cider to a new jug or carboy to remove it from the sediment and any active yeast that might still be lingering there. Next, add the sulfites (one crushed Campden tablet per gallon), and wait 24 hours. Now follow up with the potassium sorbate at a rate of ½ teaspoon per gallon. Wait

another day or two, then sweeten to taste using apple juice, apple juice concentrate, sugar, honey, or any other sweetener. Add the sweetener directly to the jug or carboy, tasting as you go using a wine thief until you're happy with the flavor.

Over the next week, keep a close eye on your cider and watch for any signs that fermentation has started again (like bubbles in the air lock). This method of neutralizing the yeast is fairly reliable, but errant yeast strains do occasionally survive the process. If you see no signs of refermentation, then you can bottle as normal. If it seems like fermentation has started again, let it carry out (it's very hard to halt an active fermentation), and then either try stabilizing your cider with sulfites and potassium sorbate a second time, or just accept what you've got.

BACK-SWEETENING WITH PASTEURIZATION

A second option is to pasteurize your finished cider. At low temperatures, you can kill the yeast without affecting the alcohol content or changing the flavor too much. To do this, sweeten the cider to taste using apple juice, apple juice concentrate, sugar, honey, or any other sweetener, and then immediately transfer it to bottles. Before capping, place all the bottles in a stockpot filled with water up to the neck (work in batches if your pot is too small).

Set the stockpot over medium heat and warm until the cider inside the center bottle registers 160°F on an instant-read thermometer. Turn the heat to low and hold the temperature of the cider at 160°F for 5 minutes to pasteurize. This is slightly longer than necessary, but adds some insurance to the process. Remove the cider from the water and cool completely before capping.

If you back-sweeten after using stabilizers (potassium metabisulfite and sorbate) or after pasteurizing your cider, you will be limited to making a still (nonsparkling) cider. As we will learn in the next section, you need a little yeast to make a bottled sparkling cider, and both of these back-sweetening methods destroy all the active yeast. (And if you add new yeast, it would consume all the sugar you just added.) While it is possible to pasteurize capped bottles of sparkling

cider, I feel that the risk of the pressurized bottles shattering during the process is too great and I don't recommend it.

STEP 7 // bottle your cider

Now, at long last, we come to the end of the cider-making process. It's time to transfer your finished cider into bottles where it will be safe from light and oxygen until you're ready to drink it.

SANITIZE YOUR BOTTLES

You'll need about ten 12-ounce bottles if you made a 1-gallon batch or about fifty 12-ounce bottles if you made a 5-gallon batch, or the equivalent number of 22-ounce bottles, 16-ounce swing-top bottles, or another bottle size. (By the way, you'll have less total volume at this point than when you started. Some cider is inevitably lost to evaporation, sampling, and user error during the cider-making process, which is poetically called "the angel's share.")

Wash all your bottles and submerge them in sanitizer solution. Place them upside down in an empty dish drainer or dishwasher rack to drain. Also sanitize all your bottle caps and place them on a clean dishtowel until needed.

Place the jug or carboy of cider on your kitchen counter. If a lot of sediment has collected in the bottom of the jug over the last few weeks, or if you used a lot of add-ins that are floating around in the jug, siphon the cider into a sanitized bucket or stockpot to separate it from the solids, and then proceed with bottling from there. This helps prevent transferring too much sediment to the bottles.

CHECK THE FINAL GRAVITY AND CALCULATE THE ALCOHOL

Before you start bottling, siphon a little cider into your hydrometer testing tube so you can check the final gravity (FG). Once you have the final gravity reading, you can compare it to your original gravity reading and calculate the alcohol by volume using this formula:

(FINAL GRAVITY—ORIGINAL GRAVITY) X 131.25 = ALCOHOL BY VOLUME PERCENT

Pour the sample back into your cider or drink it.

ADD PRIMING SUGAR FOR A SPARKLING CIDER

At this point, you have the choice of making either a still (nonsparkling) cider or a fizzy (sparkling) cider. If you want to make a still cider, you can jump straight into bottling. If you want to make a sparkling cider, you'll first need to mix a small amount of additional sugar, called "priming sugar," into your cider. This may be corn sugar, cane sugar, honey, or maple syrup, and is like one last bedtime snack for the yeast once it is in the bottle. The yeast eats this sugar, creating carbon dioxide and alcohol as usual, but now the carbon dioxide stays trapped in the bottle. This carbon dioxide is what carbonates the cider and makes it fizzy.

The amount of priming sugar needs to be very specifically measured, preferably by weight (grams or ounces). Add too little and your cider will barely sparkle. Add too much, and you'll create too much carbonation. Too little carbonation is disappointing, but not really a problem. Overcarbonation will result in a gushing geyser of cider when you open the bottle or, worse, bottles that burst once too much pressure builds inside.

For a 1-gallon batch of cider (as measured at the start of fermentation), I typically use 25 grams of corn sugar, 22 grams of cane sugar, or 50 grams of either honey or maple syrup. Scale these amounts up for larger batches. This will give you a moderately fizzy cider—enough to make the cider taste refreshing, but not so much that you get a belly full of bubbles.

To make it easier to mix the sugar into the cider, warm ¼ cup of water (or 1 cup for 5-gallon batches), add the priming sugar, and stir until dissolved. You can pour this sugar-water directly into the jug or carboy and swirl to mix. If you've siphoned your cider to a sanitized bucket or stockpot, just pour the sugar-water over the top and use a sanitized spatula to gently stir it in without splashing (or add the sugar-water to the empty bucket before siphoning the cider on top, which I prefer since I think this does the most thorough job of mixing).

One last note before we get into the mechanics of bottling: If you've aged your cider for more than three months, add some fresh yeast along with the sugar-water. With aged ciders, there's sometimes not enough active yeast left in the cider to carbonate. Add a half package of yeast for a 1-gallon batch or a full packet for a 5-gallon batch. (Do not add yeast if you've back-sweetened your cider with a fermentable sugar like honey or table sugar; the yeast will consume all the sugar you've added and possibly result in bursting bottles.)

BOTTLE THE CIDER

When you're ready to bottle, arrange all the bottles on the floor below the cider. I usually place the bottles on a baking sheet or inside a plastic bin to contain the inevitable splashes. Sanitize your autosiphon, tubing, and the bottle filler. Attach one end of the tubing to the autosiphon and the other end to the bottle filler.

Slip the autosiphon into the cider. Insert the bottle filler into the first bottle so that the tip presses against the bottom. Pump the autosiphon a few times to start the flow of cider. Some bottle fillers require you to be actively pressing the tip of the filler against the bottom of the bottle, which makes it tricky to pump the siphon at the same time; if you can, ask a friend to help.

Fill each bottle until the cider reaches the very top of the bottle, then lift the bottle filler out. The filler will automatically stop siphoning as soon as you lift it, and it will leave behind the ideal amount of headroom at the top of the bottle. (Headroom is that little bit of air at the top of the bottle between the liquid and the cap; you need an inch or two for proper carbonation.) Move on to the next bottle, and continue until all your cider has been transferred to bottles.

CAP YOUR BOTTLES

Transfer the filled bottles to the counter, and one at a time, cap each bottle. If you're using a butterfly capper, you do this by placing the cap on the top of the bottle and lowering the capper on top. Gently press down on the handles on either side of the capper until they are perpendicular to the counter. This will crimp the cap closed around the lip of the bottle and seal the bottle.

Label each bottle with the name and date of your cider, and you're done! I usually make labels out of masking tape, or I use a permanent marker to write on the caps.

STEP 8 // store your cider

Store your bottles somewhere out of direct sunlight and where the temperature is steady, like a cupboard, closet, or basement shelf. If you've made sparkling cider, wait about two weeks before opening your first bottle to give the cider time to carbonate. Still ciders can be consumed as soon as you wish, though you may notice some muted flavors in the first few weeks; this is a temporary condition called "bottle shock." Sparkling ciders should be chilled before opening, and still ciders can be consumed either at room temperature or chilled.

Ciders also keep very well and often continue to get better with time. All ciders will keep for at least a year, but I've unearthed homemade ciders that were several years old and still superb.

advanced cider techniques

Build on your cider-making skills with any of these techniques. They all start with the same base method for making cider, but add an extra twist along the way.

FLAVORING YOUR CIDER

Although perfectly good on its own, cider is also a great base for adding all sorts of flavorful ingredients, from fresh fruit to baking spices. Check out Cider-Flavoring Ingredients, starting on page 32, for some ideas.

The very best moment to add any of these extra ingredients is after the initial active stage of fermentation is complete. By this point, there's enough alcohol in the cider to protect it from most bacteria or other organisms you might accidentally introduce along with the ingredient. The alcohol also helps to pull the flavors and aromas from the ingredient and fix them in the cider, resulting in overall better flavor.

Most ingredients can be added directly to the jug or carboy any time during the second stage of fermentation. To make ingredients easy to remove after infusing, place them in a mesh bag and then knot a piece of unflavored floss or thin plastic twine around the bag. Let the long end of the floss hang out the top of the jug or bucket. Seal the jug or bucket as normal, trapping the floss beneath the jug stopper or bucket lid (unless your floss or twine is very thick, the jug or bucket should still create a tight seal). Taste the cider regularly using a wine thief and once it has infused to your liking, pull the bag of ingredients out using the floss. Alternatively, you can use any tool with a hook to remove the bag, bottle the cider immediately, or siphon the cider to a fresh jug or carboy to separate it from the ingredients.

If you're adding more than a cup or two of fresh fruit or any other ingredient, I recommend adding it about a week after fermentation has begun while the cider is still in the primary fermentation bucket. The bucket has more space for the extra volume (it can be a tight fit in the jug or carboy), and its wide opening makes it much easier to add the ingredient and separate it from the cider later on. Give this two to four weeks to infuse, and then siphon the cider to the jug or carboy.

You can also infuse your cider before fermentation begins, though you often lose some of the more delicate flavors and aromas over the course of the fermentation process. On the plus side, this is a good approach to use if you're aiming for softer, milder flavors in the finished cider.

When adding ingredients before fermentation starts, you'll need to sanitize them to make sure you don't introduce any outside contaminants. If you're treating your juice with sulfites, just add your extra ingredients at the same time and they will all be sanitized together. If you're not using sulfites, combine the ingredients in a saucepan with enough juice to cover them, bring the juice to a boil over medium-high heat, and boil for five minutes. Cool to room temperature, then add everything to the fermentation bucket along with the rest of the juice.

Lastly, you can mix any type of fruit juice with your apple juice to make a fruit cider. Blend the juices in whatever ratio you desire and ferment them together in one batch.

MAKING NATURALLY SWEET, LOW-ALCOHOL CIDERS

I won't lie: making a naturally sweet, low-alcohol cider is extremely tricky. Yeast *loves* sugar, and it's extremely difficult to convince it to stop eating all the sugar in sight. As we've talked about in previous sections, this is why most ciders end up about 7 percent alcohol and quite dry (the opposite of sweet).

Perhaps the easiest way to make a sweet cider is to add the yeast, let it ferment for a few days until you're happy with the flavor and the alcohol level, and then immediately transfer it to the refrigerator. You could even do this right in the jug the juice came in (just be sure to unscrew the cap every so often to let the carbon dioxide escape). Once refrigerated, the cold temperatures will slow the fermentation nearly to a halt, and you'll have a very refreshing, semicarbonated, low-alcohol beverage to enjoy. The cider will continue to very slowly ferment even in the fridge, so be sure to drink it within a week.

A second option for making a sweet cider is to go through the entire cider-making process as usual, wait until fermentation is complete, and then neutralize the yeast either with stabilizers (potassium metabisulfite and sorbate) or through pasteurization, as described in Adjusting the Sweetness, page 51. Once you've done this, simply add as much fresh apple juice as you like to sweeten the cider and dilute its alcohol content. Be sure to use pasteurized apple juice here since raw juice contains wild yeast and will eventually begin to ferment. Check out the Cheater's Cidre Doux on page 164 for a full recipe using this method.

A third method is to make the environment in the cider less than ideal for the yeast, which forces fermentation to stop before all the sugars have been consumed. Skip the yeast nutrients at the start of fermentation and then ferment at as low a temperature as you can manage, ideally around 55°F. This starves the yeast and makes it extremely sluggish. Once the cider is actively fermenting, if slowly, siphon it off of the sediment and into a new container once every week to slowly decrease the population of active yeast.

After a few weeks of this, fermentation will gradually come to a halt before all the sugars have been consumed. Once the gravity remains steady for several weeks in a row, your cider is done. Fermentation can start again if the cider becomes warm, so it's best to keep bottles chilled at all times and consume the cider within a few months. For a full recipe using this technique, take a look at French-Style Cidre Doux on page 163.

A final option exists, but it is difficult to do on a home cider-making level. The technique is called "keeving," and it's the method traditionally used by French cider makers to make their naturally sweet, low-alcohol cider (called *cidre doux*). If you're interested in this method and want to experiment, I suggest picking up a copy of *The New Cider Maker's Handbook* by Claude Jolicoeur. His explanation and method for keeving is unsurpassed.

MAKING APPLE WINES

Apple wine is really just regular cider that's been given a boost of fermentable sugar at the start of fermentation. The sugar increases the alcohol content above the normal range for cider, thus turning it into wine (see chapter 9, Apple Wines, for recipes).

Any kind of sugar can be used to make apple wine. Regular cane sugar ferments without leaving much flavor, so it's a good choice if you'd like to highlight the apples in your wine. Honey, maple syrup, brown sugar, and other more robustly flavored sweeteners will all leave a little of their flavor behind in the cider, which can be fantastic when making dessert wines or any wine where a touch of perceived sweetness is desired.

Add the sugar at the start of fermentation. (For the amount of sugar, see individual recipes.) To make sure it's mixed into the juice, warm the sugar with a few cups of juice in the microwave or on the stove and stir until dissolved. Cool and pour this back in with the rest

of the juice. Apple wine can take longer to ferment than regular cider, and it also benefits from a long aging period before bottling. It's good to taste your apple wine all through this time, but wait to truly judge it until at least six months after the start. Even then, the flavors often continue to improve for years.

There is such a thing as adding too much sugar. Most wine yeast hits its tolerance limit once the wine reaches 15 percent or so alcohol by volume. This means that any sugar still left in the wine at that point will remain unfermented. This is great news if your aim is a sweet dessert wine, but less ideal if you were hoping for something closer to a Pinot Grigio. Use the recipes as a starting point for your own experiments.

BLENDING FINISHED CIDERS

Blending finished ciders before bottling is something that professional cider makers do all the time. This is how they make a consistent product and also how they create new ciders with particular characteristics. We can do this at home as well.

Imagine you have one cider that finished a little more tart than you'd hoped and another cider with great apple flavor but not much else. Blend them together and voilà! Now you have a cider that has the best of both. This is also a great strategy if you come across a new variety of apple and you're not sure how it will taste in a cider. Ferment the juice from that apple on its own, see how it develops, and then blend it with other finished ciders as needed.

Before you jump in to any actual blending, make a test batch to check the ratios. Start by using a wine thief to pull small samples of each cider and mix them together in a glass. Be sure to take notes on how much of each cider you're adding. Taste the cider and keep adjusting until you're happy with the blend. Then return to the ciders themselves, blend them together according to your notes, and bottle.

beginner ciders

If this is your first time making cider and you're feeling a little nervous about the whole endeavor, start with the recipes in this chapter. These recipes build one on top of the next, and together, they will introduce you to all the different ways you can make cider at home. Most of the recipes also use apples and juice that are easily and cheaply found at any grocery store. These low stakes mean that it's okay if you make a few mistakes here and there.

But don't think that this means the cider you make will be in any way subpar to other recipes in this book! The recipes in this chapter are the ones I return to whenever I want something simple to make and easy to drink, which is often.

BASIC APPLE CIDER
average abv: 6 to 8%

This is the most basic, everyday cider that you can make. No frills, no special tricks, just a solidly good cider. Use any apple juice you like, taste it frequently during fermentation, and then adjust it, if needed, using acid blend and wine tannin when you get close to bottling. English ale yeast makes a cider with a mellow character and good apple flavor. If you like ciders that are more crisp and dry, try a white wine yeast like Montrachet or Côte des Blancs instead. When confident in your cider-making skills, use this recipe as a base for adding fruit, spices, hops, or any other flavoring you like.

1 GALLON	INGREDIENTS	5 GALLONS
1 gal (3.8 L)	APPLE JUICE	5 gal (18.9 L)
1	CAMPDEN TABLET, IF NEEDED	5
½ pkg	ENGLISH ALE OR CIDER YEAST	1 pkg
½ tsp	PECTIC ENZYME POWDER	2½ tsp
Pkg instructions	YEAST NUTRIENT	Pkg instructions
½ to 1 tsp	POWDERED ACID BLEND, IF NEEDED	2½ to 5 tsp
⅛ to ½ tsp	POWDERED WINE TANNIN, IF NEEDED	¾ to 2½ tsp
3 Tbsp (25 g)	CORN SUGAR, FOR BOTTLING	Scant 1 c (125 g)
¼ c (60ml)	HOT WATER, FOR BOTTLING	1 c (240 ml)

Pour the juice into a sanitized fermentation bucket. Check and record the original gravity. (If using unpasteurized juice, crush the Campden tablet[s] and whisk into the juice; snap on the lid, insert an air lock filled with sanitizer or vodka, and let the juice stand for 24 hours.)

Sprinkle the yeast, pectic enzyme, and yeast nutrient over the juice. Whisk vigorously with a sanitized whisk to dissolve the ingredients and aerate the juice. Snap on the lid and insert a filled air lock. Place the bucket out of direct sunlight and at room temperature (70° to 75°F). Fermentation should begin within 24 hours (bubbles will pop regularly through the air lock). Active fermentation will peak after a few days, then gradually finish within 1 to 2 weeks.

Once you've seen very little activity in the air lock for a few days (a stray bubble or two is fine), siphon the cider to a sanitized jug or carboy, leaving behind as much sediment as possible. As you transfer the cider, taste it using a sanitized wine thief to check its progress. Insert the stopper and air lock, then place the cider out of direct sunlight and at room temperature for another 2 weeks or up to 2 months.

When ready to bottle, taste the cider again. If needed, add acid blend for more acidity or tannin for more astringency. Taste again a few days later, and continue adjusting and tasting until you're happy.

Check the final gravity and calculate the ABV. Dissolve the corn sugar in the hot water and mix with the cider, back-sweetening if desired (see page 52). Bottle the cider. Wait 2 weeks before drinking or store for up to a year. Serve chilled.

A TOUCH SWEET CIDER

average abv: 6 to 8%

To make a cider that still has a touch of natural sweetness, I like to add some pear juice to the mix. Pear juice has a milder, less-acidic flavor after going through fermentation, and this helps soften the edges on a cider without changing its essential nature. If you're buying pear juice at the store, make sure you're buying bottles labeled 100 percent pear juice. Pear juice can often have a lot of sediment, so you may end up losing some volume when you transfer it to your jug or carboy. Top it off with more pear juice or apple juice if needed and then let the extra juice ferment before bottling.

1 GALLON	INGREDIENTS	5 GALLONS
3 qt (2.8 L)	APPLE JUICE	3¾ gal (14.2 L)
1 qt (0.9 L)	PEAR JUICE	1¼ gal (4.7 L)
1	CAMPDEN TABLET, IF NEEDED	5
½ pkg	ENGLISH ALE OR CIDER YEAST	1 pkg
½ tsp	PECTIC ENZYME POWDER	2½ tsp
Pkg instructions	YEAST NUTRIENT	Pkg instructions
½ to 1 tsp	POWDERED ACID BLEND, IF NEEDED	2½ to 5 tsp
⅛ to ½ tsp	POWDERED WINE TANNIN, IF NEEDED	¾ to 2½ tsp
3 Tbsp (25 g)	CORN SUGAR, FOR BOTTLING	Scant 1 c (125 g)
¼ c (60ml)	HOT WATER, FOR BOTTLING	1 c (240 ml)

Pour the juices into a sanitized fermentation bucket. Check and record the original gravity. (If using unpasteurized juice, crush the Campden tablet[s] and whisk into the juice; snap on the lid, insert an air lock filled with sanitizer or vodka, and let the juice stand for 24 hours.)

Sprinkle the yeast, pectic enzyme, and yeast nutrient over the juice. Whisk vigorously with a sanitized whisk to dissolve the ingredients and aerate the juice. Snap on the lid and insert a filled air lock. Place the bucket out of direct sunlight and at room temperature (70° to 75°F). Fermentation should begin within 24 hours (bubbles will pop regularly through the air lock). Active fermentation will peak after a few days, and then gradually finish within 1 to 2 weeks.

Once you've seen very little activity in the air lock for a few days (a stray bubble or two is fine), siphon the cider to a sanitized jug or carboy, leaving behind as much sediment as possible. As you transfer the cider, taste it using a sanitized wine thief to check its progress. Insert the stopper and air lock, then place the cider out of direct sunlight and at room temperature (70° to 75°F) for another 2 weeks or up to 2 months before bottling.

When ready to bottle, taste the cider again. If needed, add acid blend for more acidity or tannin for more astringency. Taste again a few days later, and continue adjusting and tasting until you're happy.

Check the final gravity and calculate the ABV. Dissolve the corn sugar in the hot water and mix with the cider, back-sweetening if desired (see page 52). Bottle the cider. Wait 2 weeks before drinking or store for up to a year. Serve chilled.

SUPERMARKET CIDER

average abv: 6 to 8%

This cider, as well as the following two recipes, are minor variations of the Basic Apple Cider (page 64). The only real difference is the kind of apple juice you'll be using. I want to walk you through this series of recipes to get you thinking about all the different kinds and sources of apple juice available to you. This recipe starts you out with the cheapest, most basic, and least fancy supermarket juice you can find. And you know what? It's really good! You might not win any awards for this cider, but for something fun and bubbly to drink at day's end, it's perfect. Don't worry if the juice has preservatives; most commercial yeast strains are hardy enough to still provide a good fermentation.

1 GALLON	INGREDIENTS	5 GALLONS
1 gal (3.8 L)	APPLE JUICE	5 gal (18.9 L)
1	CAMPDEN TABLET, IF NEEDED	5
½ pkg	ENGLISH ALE OR CIDER YEAST	1 pkg
½ tsp	PECTIC ENZYME POWDER	2½ tsp
Pkg instructions	YEAST NUTRIENT	Pkg instructions
½ to 1 tsp	POWDERED ACID BLEND, IF NEEDED	2½ to 5 tsp
⅛ to ½ tsp	POWDERED WINE TANNIN, IF NEEDED	¾ to 2½ tsp
3 Tbsp (25 g)	CORN SUGAR, FOR BOTTLING	Scant 1 c (125 g)
¼ c (60ml)	HOT WATER, FOR BOTTLING	1 c (240 ml)

Pour the juice into a sanitized fermentation bucket. Check and record the original gravity. (If using unpasteurized juice, crush the Campden tablet[s] and whisk into the juice; snap on the lid, insert an air lock filled with sanitizer or vodka, and let the juice stand for 24 hours.)

Sprinkle the yeast, pectic enzyme, and yeast nutrient over the juice. Whisk vigorously with a sanitized whisk to dissolve the ingredients and aerate the juice. Snap on the lid and insert a filled air lock. Place the bucket out of direct sunlight and at room temperature (70° to 75°F). Fermentation should begin within 24 hours (bubbles will pop regularly through the air lock). Active fermentation will peak after a few days, and then gradually finish within 1 to 2 weeks.

Once you've seen very little activity in the air lock for a few days (a stray bubble or two is fine), siphon the cider to a sanitized jug or carboy, leaving behind as much sediment as possible. As you transfer the cider, taste it using a sanitized wine thief to check its progress. Insert the stopper and air lock, then place the cider out of direct sunlight and at room temperature for another 2 weeks or up to 2 months.

When ready to bottle, taste the cider again. If needed, add acid blend for more acidity or tannin for more astringency. Taste again a few days later, and continue adjusting and tasting until you're happy.

Check the final gravity and calculate the ABV. Dissolve the corn sugar in the hot water and mix with the cider, back-sweetening if desired (see page 52). Bottle the cider. Wait 2 weeks before drinking or store for up to a year. Serve chilled.

BETTER SUPERMARKET CIDER
average abv: 6 to 8%

Okay, let's help our Supermarket Cider (page 67) mature a little. Instead of using the most basic, mass-produced juice, dig a little deeper into the shelves and refrigerators at your grocery store. I bet you'll be surprised at the variety of juices you'll find: pressings of single-variety apples, organic and preservative-free juices from small producers, reasonably fresh apple juice in the refrigerated section. Explore markets outside your chain grocery store and see what they have to offer. Grab a few different kinds that sound good and blend them together—after all, a good cider is all about the blend.

1 GALLON	INGREDIENTS	5 GALLONS
1 gal (3.8 L)	APPLE JUICE	5 gal (18.9 L)
1	CAMPDEN TABLET, IF NEEDED	5
½ pkg	ENGLISH ALE OR CIDER YEAST	1 pkg
½ tsp	PECTIC ENZYME POWDER	2½ tsp
Pkg instructions	YEAST NUTRIENT	Pkg instructions
½ to 1 tsp	POWDERED ACID BLEND, IF NEEDED	2½ to 5 tsp
⅛ to ½ tsp	POWDERED WINE TANNIN, IF NEEDED	¾ to 2½ tsp
3 Tbsp (25 g)	CORN SUGAR, FOR BOTTLING	Scant 1 c (125 g)
¼ c (60ml)	HOT WATER, FOR BOTTLING	1 c (240 ml)

Pour the juice into a sanitized fermentation bucket. Check and record the original gravity. (If using unpasteurized juice, crush the Campden tablet[s] and whisk into the juice; snap on the lid, insert an air lock filled with sanitizer or vodka, and let the juice stand for 24 hours.)

Sprinkle the yeast, pectic enzyme, and yeast nutrient over the juice. Whisk vigorously with a sanitized whisk to dissolve the ingredients and aerate the juice. Snap on the lid and insert a filled air lock. Place the bucket out of direct sunlight and at room temperature (70° to 75°F). Fermentation should begin within 24 hours (bubbles will pop regularly through the air lock). Active fermentation will peak after a few days, and then gradually finish within 1 to 2 weeks.

Once you've seen very little activity in the air lock for a few days (a stray bubble or two is fine), siphon the cider to a sanitized jug or carboy, leaving behind as much sediment as possible. As you transfer the cider, taste it using a sanitized wine thief to check its progress. Insert the stopper and air lock, then place the cider out of direct sunlight and at room temperature for another 2 weeks or up to 2 months.

When ready to bottle, taste the cider again. If needed, add acid blend for more acidity or tannin for more astringency. Taste again a few days later, and continue adjusting and tasting until you're happy.

Check the final gravity and calculate the ABV. Dissolve the corn sugar in the hot water and mix with the cider, back-sweetening if desired (see page 52). Bottle the cider. Wait 2 weeks before drinking or store for up to a year. Serve chilled.

FARMERS' MARKET CIDER

average abv: 6 to 8%

For our final variation on Basic Apple Cider (page 64), seek out true fresh-pressed cider at the farmers' market or a nearby orchard. This means you will likely need to wait until fall to make this cider, which is when apples—and thus fresh apple juice—are in season. If you can, taste the juice before you buy it and ask about the blend of apples used in the juice. This is how you start training yourself to recognize the link between apples, how they taste once juiced, and their flavor in your finished cider.

1 GALLON	INGREDIENTS	5 GALLONS
1 gal (3.8 L)	APPLE JUICE	5 gal (18.9 L)
1	CAMPDEN TABLET, IF NEEDED	5
½ pkg	ENGLISH ALE OR CIDER YEAST	1 pkg
½ tsp	PECTIC ENZYME POWDER	2½ tsp
Pkg instructions	YEAST NUTRIENT	Pkg instructions
½ to 1 tsp	POWDERED ACID BLEND, IF NEEDED	2½ to 5 tsp
⅛ to ½ tsp	POWDERED WINE TANNIN, IF NEEDED	¾ to 2½ tsp
3 Tbsp (25 g)	CORN SUGAR, FOR BOTTLING	Scant 1 c (125 g)
¼ c (60ml)	HOT WATER, FOR BOTTLING	1 c (240 ml)

Pour the juice into a sanitized fermentation bucket. Check and record the original gravity. (If using unpasteurized juice, crush the Campden tablet[s] and whisk into the juice; snap on the lid, insert an air lock filled with sanitizer or vodka, and let the juice stand for 24 hours.)

Sprinkle the yeast, pectic enzyme, and yeast nutrient over the juice. Whisk vigorously with a sanitized whisk to dissolve the ingredients and aerate the juice. Snap on the lid and insert a filled air lock. Place the bucket out of direct sunlight and at room temperature (70° to 75°F). Fermentation should begin within 24 hours (bubbles will pop regularly through the air lock). Active fermentation will peak after a few days, and then gradually finish within 1 to 2 weeks.

Once you've seen very little activity in the air lock for a few days (a stray bubble or two is fine), siphon the cider to a sanitized jug or carboy, leaving behind as much sediment as possible. As you transfer the cider, taste it using a sanitized wine thief to check its progress. Insert the stopper and air lock, then place the cider out of direct sunlight and at room temperature for another 2 weeks or up to 2 months.

When ready to bottle, taste the cider again. If needed, add acid blend for more acidity or tannin for more astringency. Taste again a few days later, and continue adjusting and tasting until you're happy.

Check the final gravity and calculate the ABV. Dissolve the corn sugar in the hot water and mix with the cider, back-sweetening if desired (see page 52). Bottle the cider. Wait 2 weeks before drinking or store for up to a year. Serve chilled.

OLD GRANNY FRESH-PRESSED CIDER

average abv: 6 to 8%

The next step up from buying your apple juice is pressing it yourself. This cider uses a mix of inexpensive apples easily found at most grocery stores, so it's a good one to make first as you get a feel for pressing your own juice—small investment, big reward! Granny Smith apples have a solid and fairly consistent acid level, and their juice makes a good base for cider. Gala, Fuji, and Golden Delicious apples bring in some extra sugar and good apple flavor, or use a mix of any sweet apples you like. You will likely need to add some tannin at the end to balance the other flavors in the cider. Wait until close to bottling, taste the cider, then adjust as needed.

You'll need a juicer or an apple press for this recipe. If you're not ready to buy either for yourself, see if you can borrow one from a friend or someone at a local homebrewing club.

1 GALLON	INGREDIENTS	5 GALLONS
13 lb (5.9 kg)	GRANNY SMITH APPLES	65 lb (29.5 kg)
7 lb (3.2 kg)	MIX OF GALA, FUJI & GOLDEN DELICIOUS APPLES	35 lb (15.9 kg)
1	CAMPDEN TABLET	5
½ pkg	ENGLISH ALE OR CIDER YEAST	1 pkg
½ tsp	PECTIC ENZYME POWDER	2½ tsp
Pkg instructions	YEAST NUTRIENT	Pkg instructions
½ to 1 tsp	POWDERED ACID BLEND, IF NEEDED	2½ to 5 tsp
⅛ to ½ tsp	POWDERED WINE TANNIN, IF NEEDED	¾ to 2½ tsp
3 Tbsp (25 g)	CORN SUGAR, FOR BOTTLING	Scant 1 c (125 g)
¼ c (60ml)	HOT WATER, FOR BOTTLING	1 c (240 ml)

Wash all the apples and trim away any large bruises or damaged bits. Juice or press the apples as described in "Press Your Own Apples" (page 16).

Pour the juice into a sanitized fermentation bucket. Check and record the original gravity. Crush the Campden tablet(s) and whisk into the juice; snap on the lid, insert an air lock filled with sanitizer or vodka, and let the juice stand for 24 hours.

Sprinkle the yeast, pectic enzyme, and yeast nutrient over the juice. Whisk vigorously with a sanitized whisk to dissolve the ingredients and aerate the juice. Snap on the lid and insert a filled air lock. Place the bucket out of direct sunlight and at room temperature (70° to 75°F). Fermentation should begin within 24 hours (bubbles will pop regularly through the air lock). Active fermentation will peak after a few days, and then gradually finish within 1 to 2 weeks.

Once you've seen very little activity in the air lock for a few days (a stray bubble or two is fine), siphon the cider to a sanitized jug or carboy, leaving behind as much sediment as possible. As you transfer the cider, taste it using a sanitized wine thief to check its progress. Insert the stopper and air lock, then place the cider out of direct sunlight and at room temperature for another 2 weeks or up to 2 months.

When ready to bottle, taste the cider again. If needed, add acid blend for more acidity or tannin for more astringency. Taste again a few days later, and continue adjusting and tasting until you're happy.

Check the final gravity and calculate the ABV. Dissolve the corn sugar in the hot water and mix with the cider, back-sweetening if desired (see page 52). Bottle the cider. Wait 2 weeks before drinking or store for up to a year. Serve chilled.

SINGLE-VARIETY FRESH-PRESSED CIDER

average abv: 6 to 8%

The very best ciders usually blend several varieties of apples, which unite to make a balanced cider. However, a handful of apple varieties make a good cider all on their own: Gravenstein, Mutsu, McIntosh, and Baldwin are a few of the most common. Ciders made from these apples shouldn't need much acid or tannin, but the emphasis is on "should." Taste the cider after fermenting and add acid or tannin if you think it needs help— use your best judgment.

Making a small batch of a single apple variety is also a great way to see how a new-to-you apple tastes when made into cider. Press a gallon or so of juice from this apple, let it ferment, and taste it when it's done. If you like it, drink it on its own; otherwise, mix it with other single-variety ciders to make your own signature blend.

1 GALLON	INGREDIENTS	5 GALLONS
20 lb (9 kg)	SINGLE-VARIETY APPLES, LIKE GRAVENSTEIN OR MUTSU	100 lb (45 kg)
1	CAMPDEN TABLET	5
½ pkg	ENGLISH ALE OR CIDER YEAST	1 pkg
½ tsp	PECTIC ENZYME POWDER	2½ tsp
Pkg instructions	YEAST NUTRIENT	Pkg instructions
½ to 1 tsp	POWDERED ACID BLEND, IF NEEDED	2½ to 5 tsp
⅛ to ½ tsp	POWDERED WINE TANNIN, IF NEEDED	¾ to 2½ tsp
3 Tbsp (25 g)	CORN SUGAR, FOR BOTTLING	Scant 1 c (125 g)
¼ c (60ml)	HOT WATER, FOR BOTTLING	1 c (240 ml)

Wash all the apples and trim away any large bruises or damaged bits. Juice or press the apples as described in "Press Your Own Apples" (page 16).

Pour the juice into a sanitized fermentation bucket. Check and record the original gravity. Crush the Campden tablet(s) and whisk into the juice; snap on the lid, insert an air lock filled with sanitizer or vodka, and let the juice stand for 24 hours.

Sprinkle the yeast, pectic enzyme, and yeast nutrient over the juice. Whisk vigorously with a sanitized whisk to dissolve the ingredients and aerate the juice. Snap on the lid and insert a filled air lock. Place the bucket out of direct sunlight and at room temperature (70° to 75°F). Fermentation should begin within 24 hours (bubbles will pop regularly through the air lock). Active fermentation will peak after a few days, and then gradually finish within 1 to 2 weeks.

Once you've seen very little activity in the air lock for a few days (a stray bubble or two is fine), siphon the cider to a sanitized jug or carboy, leaving behind as much sediment as possible. As you transfer the cider, taste it using a sanitized wine thief to check its progress. Insert the stopper and air lock, then place the cider out of direct sunlight and at room temperature for another 2 weeks or up to 2 months.

When ready to bottle, taste the cider again. If needed, add acid blend for more acidity or tannin for more astringency. Taste again a few days later, and continue adjusting and tasting until you're happy.

Check the final gravity and calculate the ABV. Dissolve the corn sugar in the hot water and mix with the cider, back-sweetening if desired (see page 52). Bottle the cider. Wait 2 weeks before drinking or store for up to a year. Serve chilled.

TRADITIONAL FRESH-PRESSED CIDER
average abv: 6 to 8%

Wait to make this cider until apple season is well underway so that you have plenty of varieties to choose from. Peruse the farmers' market or find a local orchard with a large selection of apples, and take liberal advantage of samples. You're looking for a good mix of sweet, acidic, and bitter apples. You want at least one kind of apple from each category. If you're struggling to find the bitter component, look for crabapples and quince, which are more widely available. In your final mix, you want 30 to 60 percent sweet apples, 10 to 20 percent acidic apples, and 5 to 20 percent bitter apples. Take a look at the Apples for Cider chart on page 13 for some good varieties.

1 GALLON	INGREDIENTS	5 GALLONS
18 to 20 lb (8 to 9 kg)	APPLES, MIXED VARIETIES	90 to 100 lb (40 to 45 kg)
1	CAMPDEN TABLET	5
½ pkg	ENGLISH ALE OR CIDER YEAST	1 pkg
½ tsp	PECTIC ENZYME POWDER	2½ tsp
Pkg instructions	YEAST NUTRIENT	Pkg instructions
½ to 1 tsp	POWDERED ACID BLEND, IF NEEDED	2½ to 5 tsp
⅛ to ½ tsp	POWDERED WINE TANNIN, IF NEEDED	¾ to 2½ tsp
3 Tbsp (25 g)	CORN SUGAR, FOR BOTTLING	Scant 1 c (125 g)
¼ c (60ml)	HOT WATER, FOR BOTTLING	1 c (240 ml)

Wash all the apples and trim away any large bruises or damaged bits. Juice or press the apples as described in "Press Your Own Apples" (page 16).

Pour the juice into a sanitized fermentation bucket. Check and record the original gravity. Crush the Campden tablet(s) and whisk into the juice; snap on the lid, insert an air lock filled with sanitizer or vodka, and let the juice stand for 24 hours.

Sprinkle the yeast, pectic enzyme, and yeast nutrient over the juice. Whisk vigorously with a sanitized whisk to dissolve the ingredients and aerate the juice. Snap on the lid and insert a filled air lock. Place the bucket out of direct sunlight and at room temperature (70° to 75°F). Fermentation should begin within 24 hours (bubbles will pop regularly through the air lock). Active fermentation will peak after a few days, and then gradually finish within 1 to 2 weeks.

Once you've seen very little activity in the air lock for a few days (a stray bubble or two is fine), siphon the cider to a sanitized jug or carboy, leaving behind as much sediment as possible. As you transfer the cider, taste it using a sanitized wine thief to check its progress. Insert the stopper and air lock, then place the cider out of direct sunlight and at room temperature for another 2 weeks or up to 2 months.

When ready to bottle, taste the cider again. If needed, add acid blend for more acidity or tannin for more astringency. Taste again a few days later, and continue adjusting and tasting until you're happy.

Check the final gravity and calculate the ABV. Dissolve the corn sugar in the hot water and mix with the cider, back-sweetening if desired (see page 52). Bottle the cider. Wait 2 weeks before drinking or store for up to a year. Serve chilled.

the cider family

Two other members of the great and venerable cider family are perries and cysers. "Perries" are ciders made with pear juice instead of apple juice, and "cysers" are ciders fortified with honey.

Pears have been a part of cider making just as long as apples, but perries have dropped out of popularity in recent decades. Goodness knows why, because perries are delicious. Pears have less malic acid than apples and the tannins in the skins are of a slightly different quality. Perries also have a lot of sorbitol, which is an unfermentable sugar. As a whole, this means that perries have a softer, gentler, and more well-rounded flavor than apple-based cider, along with an almost creamy, champagne-like texture that I find irresistible.

Honey is a splendid companion to apples. This is true for desserts and it's equally true for cider. Wildflower, clover, and orange-blossom honeys add a mild floral sweetness to ciders and are widely available. It can also be fun to experiment with darker and more uniquely flavored varieties of honey like buckwheat, avocado, and chestnut.

Remember that honey is a fermentable sugar and will therefore boost the alcohol content of your cider. Be careful of adding too much or you'll wind up with an apple wine—unless that's your intention, of course! (For more on apple wines, see chapter 9.)

PERRY (PEAR CIDER)

average abv: 6 to 8%

Perry is made with fall's other favorite fruit: the pear. Just as there are bitter, tannic apples meant for cider, there are also bitter, tannic pears meant specifically for perry—but they are even harder to find than bitter apples. Instead, use whatever pears or pear juice you can find and add a little acid blend and tannin if needed to round out the flavor. Store-bought pear juice often contains a lot of pulpy sediment, which never fully compacts and can become very annoying when trying to siphon the clear perry off the top. Try to buy varieties that seem to have less pulp in the bottle and top off your jug or carboy with extra juice if you need to. Let the extra juice ferment before bottling.

1 GALLON	INGREDIENTS	5 GALLONS
1 gal (3.8 L)	PEAR JUICE	5 gal (18.9 L)
1	CAMPDEN TABLET, IF NEEDED	5
½ pkg	ENGLISH ALE OR CIDER YEAST	1 pkg
½ tsp	PECTIC ENZYME POWDER	2½ tsp
Pkg instructions	YEAST NUTRIENT	Pkg instructions
½ to 1 tsp	POWDERED ACID BLEND, IF NEEDED	2½ to 5 tsp
⅛ to ½ tsp	POWDERED WINE TANNIN, IF NEEDED	¾ to 2½ tsp
3 Tbsp (25 g)	CORN SUGAR, FOR BOTTLING	Scant 1 c (125 g)
¼ c (60ml)	HOT WATER, FOR BOTTLING	1 c (240 ml)

Pour the juice into a sanitized fermentation bucket. Check and record the original gravity. (If using unpasteurized juice, crush the Campden tablet[s] and whisk into the juice; snap on the lid, insert an air lock filled with sanitizer or vodka, and let the juice stand for 24 hours.)

Sprinkle the yeast, pectic enzyme, and yeast nutrient over the juice. Whisk vigorously with a sanitized whisk to dissolve the ingredients and aerate the juice.

Snap on the lid and insert a filled air lock. Place the bucket out of direct sunlight and at room temperature (70° to 75°F). Fermentation should begin within 24 hours (bubbles will pop regularly through the air lock). Active fermentation will peak after a few days, and then gradually finish within 1 to 2 weeks.

Once you've seen very little activity in the air lock for a few days (a stray bubble or two is fine), siphon the perry to a sanitized jug or carboy, leaving behind as much sediment as possible. As you transfer the perry, taste it using a sanitized wine thief to check its progress. Insert the stopper and air lock, then place the perry out of direct sunlight and at room temperature for another 2 weeks or up to 2 months.

When ready to bottle, taste the perry again. If needed, add acid blend for more acidity or tannin for more astringency. Taste again a few days later, and continue adjusting and tasting until you're happy.

Check the final gravity and calculate the ABV. Dissolve the corn sugar in the hot water and mix with the perry, back-sweetening if desired (see page 52). Bottle the perry. Wait 2 weeks before drinking or store for up to a year. Serve chilled.

CYSER (HONEY CIDER)

average abv: 11%

Cysers are where ciders and meads (honey wines) overlap. This one is made with apple juice and just enough honey to give it a perceptible wildflower sweetness without overwhelming the apple flavors. Add more honey if you'd like to make something closer to dessert wine. (See chapter 9, Apple Wines, for more inspiration.) I leave this cyser uncarbonated, and I like to serve it as a light table wine with dinner. If you'd like to make a cyser with some fizz, see the recipe for Crisp Sparkling Cyser (page 86).

1 GALLON	INGREDIENTS	5 GALLONS
1 gal (3.8 L)	APPLE JUICE	5 gal (18.9 L)
1 c (340 g)	HONEY, ANY VARIETY	5 c (1.7 kg)
1	CAMPDEN TABLET, IF NEEDED	5
½ pkg	WHITE WINE YEAST	1 pkg
½ tsp	PECTIC ENZYME POWDER	2½ tsp
Pkg instructions	YEAST NUTRIENT	Pkg instructions
½ to 1 tsp	POWDERED ACID BLEND, IF NEEDED	2½ to 5 tsp
⅛ to ½ tsp	POWDERED WINE TANNIN, IF NEEDED	¾ to 2½ tsp

Combine a few cups of the juice and the honey in a small saucepan. Warm over medium heat, stirring gently, until the honey has dissolved. Remove from the heat and let cool to room temperature.

Combine the honey mixture and remaining juice in a sanitized fermentation bucket. Check and record the original gravity. (If using unpasteurized juice, crush the Campden tablet[s] and whisk into the juice; snap on the lid, insert an air lock filled with sanitizer or vodka, and let the juice stand for 24 hours.)

Sprinkle the yeast, pectic enzyme, and yeast nutrient over the juice. Whisk vigorously with a sanitized whisk to dissolve the ingredients and aerate the juice. Snap on the lid and insert a filled air lock. Place the bucket out of direct sunlight and at room temperature (70° to 75°F). Fermentation should begin within 24 hours (bubbles will pop regularly through the air lock). Active fermentation will peak after a few days, and then gradually finish within 1 to 2 weeks.

Once you've seen very little activity in the air lock for a few days (a stray bubble or two is fine), siphon the cyser to a sanitized jug or carboy, leaving behind as much sediment as possible. As you transfer the cyser, taste it using a sanitized wine thief to check its progress. Insert the stopper and air lock, then place the cyser out of direct sunlight and at room temperature for another 2 weeks or up to 2 months.

When ready to bottle, taste the cyser again. If needed, add acid blend for more acidity or tannin for more astringency. Taste again a few days later, and continue adjusting and tasting until you're happy.

Check the final gravity and calculate the ABV. Bottle the cyser, back-sweetening if desired (see page 52). Wait 2 weeks before drinking or store for up to a year. Serve chilled.

VANILLA PERRY

average abv: 6 to 8%

Vanilla beans are one of my favorite "extras" to add to perries and ciders. They add an ephemeral sweetness and a floral quality, like sipping nectar. It's not so much vanilla that things tip into Yankee Candle territory, but just enough to make each sip feel special.

Buy whole vanilla beans for this perry. Make sure they are look pump and oily, not shrunken or dry. Any leftover beans should be used for another perry, cider, or baking project within a few weeks, or they start to dry out and lose their magic.

1 GALLON	INGREDIENTS	5 GALLONS
3 qt (2.8 L)	PEAR JUICE	3¾ gal (14.2 L)
1 qt (0.9 L)	APPLE JUICE	1¼ gal (4.7 L)
1	CAMPDEN TABLET, IF NEEDED	5
½ pkg	WHITE WINE YEAST	1 pkg
½ tsp	PECTIC ENZYME POWDER	2½ tsp
Pkg instructions	YEAST NUTRIENT	Pkg instructions
½	VANILLA BEAN, WHOLE	2
½ to 1 tsp	POWDERED ACID BLEND, IF NEEDED	2½ to 5 tsp
⅛ to ½ tsp	POWDERED WINE TANNIN, IF NEEDED	¾ to 2½ tsp
3 Tbsp (25 g)	CORN SUGAR, FOR BOTTLING	Scant 1 c (125 g)
¼ c (60ml)	HOT WATER, FOR BOTTLING	1 c (240 ml)

Pour the juices into a sanitized fermentation bucket. Check and record the original gravity. (If using unpasteurized juice, crush the Campden tablet[s] and whisk into the juice; snap on the lid, insert an air lock filled with sanitizer or vodka, and let the juice stand for 24 hours.)

Sprinkle the yeast, pectic enzyme, and yeast nutrient over the juice. Whisk vigorously with a sanitized whisk to dissolve the ingredients and aerate the juice. Snap on

the lid and insert a filled air lock. Place the bucket out of direct sunlight and at room temperature (70° to 75°F). Fermentation should begin within 24 hours (bubbles will pop regularly through the air lock). Active fermentation will peak after a few days, and then gradually finish within 1 to 2 weeks.

Once you've seen very little activity in the air lock for a few days (a stray bubble or two is fine), split the vanilla bean(s) and scrape out the seeds. Place both the seeds and pods in a mesh bag and place in a sanitized jug or carboy. Siphon the perry over the top, leaving behind as much sediment as possible. As you transfer the perry, taste it using a sanitized wine thief to check its progress. Insert the stopper and air lock, then place the perry out of direct sunlight and at room temperature for another 2 weeks or up to 2 months. Taste regularly and remove the vanilla bean(s) when you like the flavor (you can also add more vanilla beans for stronger flavor, if you'd like).

When ready to bottle, taste the perry again. If needed, add acid blend for more acidity or tannin for more astringency. Taste again a few days later, and continue adjusting and tasting until you're happy.

Check the final gravity and calculate the ABV. Dissolve the corn sugar in the hot water and mix with the perry, back-sweetening if desired (see page 52). Bottle the perry. Wait 2 weeks before drinking or store for up to a year. Serve chilled.

BLACK CURRANT PERRY

average abv: 6 to 8%

Black currants are small, dark-purple berries with a flavor like slightly tart, extra-concentrated grape juice. They give this perry an earthy, berry-like flavor and a pretty reddish hue. In the United States, fresh currants can be hard to find unless you grow them yourself, but dried black currants can usually be found at gourmet markets. If you do luck into some fresh black currants, by all means use them here! Crush them lightly to release their juices, then add both juice and berries to the perry once active fermentation has slowed and before transferring to the jug or carboy.

1 GALLON	INGREDIENTS	5 GALLONS
3 qt (2.8 L)	PEAR JUICE	3¾ gal (14.2 L)
1 qt (0.9 L)	APPLE JUICE	1¼ gal (4.7 L)
1	CAMPDEN TABLET, IF NEEDED	5
½ pkg	WHITE WINE YEAST	1 pkg
½ tsp	PECTIC ENZYME POWDER	2½ tsp
Pkg instructions	YEAST NUTRIENT	Pkg instructions
3 c (425 g)	DRIED BLACK CURRANTS	15 c (2.1 kg)
½ to 1 tsp	POWDERED ACID BLEND, IF NEEDED	2½ to 5 tsp
⅛ to ½ tsp	POWDERED WINE TANNIN, IF NEEDED	¾ to 2½ tsp
3 Tbsp (25 g)	CORN SUGAR, FOR BOTTLING	Scant 1 c (125 g)
¼ c (60ml)	HOT WATER, FOR BOTTLING	1 c (240 ml)

Pour the juices into a sanitized fermentation bucket. Check and record the original gravity. (If using unpasteurized juice, crush the Campden tablet[s] and whisk into the juice; snap on the lid, insert an air lock filled with sanitizer or vodka, and let the juice stand for 24 hours.)

Sprinkle the yeast, pectic enzyme, and yeast nutrient over the juice. Whisk vigorously with a sanitized whisk to dissolve the ingredients and aerate the juice. Snap on the lid and insert a filled air lock. Place the bucket out of direct sunlight and at room temperature (70° to 75°F). Fermentation should begin within 24 hours (bubbles will pop regularly through the air lock). Active fermentation will peak after a few days, and then gradually finish within 1 to 2 weeks.

Once you've seen very little activity in the air lock for a few days (a stray bubble or two is fine), measure the black currants into a mesh bag and place in a sanitized jug or carboy. Siphon the perry over the top, leaving behind as much sediment as possible. As you transfer the perry, taste it using a sanitized wine thief to check its progress. Insert the stopper and air lock, then place the perry out of direct sunlight and at room temperature for another 2 weeks or up to 2 months. Taste regularly and remove the currants when you like the flavor.

When ready to bottle, taste the perry again. If needed, add acid blend for more acidity or tannin for more astringency. Taste again a few days later, and continue adjusting and tasting until you're happy.

Check the final gravity and calculate the ABV. Dissolve the corn sugar in the hot water and mix with the perry, back-sweetening if desired (see page 52). Bottle the perry. Wait 2 weeks before drinking or store for up to a year. Serve chilled.

BUCKWHEAT CYSER

average abv: 9%

Buckwheat honey has an earthy, nutty, and somewhat bitter flavor that is the polar opposite of the mild wildflower honey that most of us are used to having with breakfast. Its flavor is so strong that it can be challenging to figure out what to do with it. On a whim, I added some to a batch of cider and was happily surprised with the caramel-like flavor that emerged a few weeks later. This cider also has a rustic quality that I love, helped along by a Belgian saison yeast strain. This cyser is excellent either still or carbonated—you pick!

1 GALLON	INGREDIENTS	5 GALLONS
1 gal (3.8 L)	APPLE JUICE	5 gal (18.9 L)
½ c (170 g)	BUCKWHEAT HONEY	2½ c (850 g)
1	CAMPDEN TABLET, IF NEEDED	5
½ pkg	BELGIAN SAISON YEAST	1 pkg
½ tsp	PECTIC ENZYME POWDER	2½ tsp
Pkg instructions	YEAST NUTRIENT	Pkg instructions
½ to 1 tsp	POWDERED ACID BLEND, IF NEEDED	2½ to 5 tsp
⅛ to ½ tsp	POWDERED WINE TANNIN, IF NEEDED	¾ to 2½ tsp
2½ Tbsp (50 g)	BUCKWHEAT HONEY, FOR BOTTLING (OPTIONAL)	Scant ¾ c (250 g)
¼ c (60ml)	HOT WATER, FOR BOTTLING (OPTIONAL)	1 c (240 ml)

Combine a few cups of the juice and the honey in a small saucepan. Warm over medium heat, stirring gently, until the honey has dissolved. Remove from the heat and let cool to room temperature.

Combine the honey mixture and remaining juice in a sanitized fermentation bucket. Check and record the original gravity. (If using unpasteurized juice, crush the Campden tablet[s] and whisk into the juice; snap on the lid, insert an air lock filled with sanitizer or vodka, and let the juice stand for 24 hours.)

Sprinkle the yeast, pectic enzyme, and yeast nutrient over the juice. Whisk vigorously with a sanitized whisk to dissolve the ingredients and aerate the juice. Snap on the lid and insert a filled air lock. Place the bucket out of direct sunlight and at room temperature (70° to 75°F). Fermentation should begin within 24 hours (bubbles will pop regularly through the air lock). Active fermentation will peak after a few days, and then gradually finish within 1 to 2 weeks.

Once you've seen very little activity in the air lock for a few days (a stray bubble or two is fine), siphon the cyser to a sanitized jug or carboy, leaving behind as much sediment as possible. As you transfer the cyser, taste it using a sanitized wine thief to check its progress. Insert the stopper and air lock, then place the cyser out of direct sunlight and at room temperature for another 2 weeks or up to 2 months.

When ready to bottle, taste the cyser again. If needed, add acid blend for more acidity or tannin for more astringency. Taste again a few days later, and continue adjusting and tasting until you're happy.

Check the final gravity and calculate the ABV. Dissolve the honey in the hot water and mix with the cyser, back-sweetening if desired (see page 52). Bottle the cyser. Wait 2 weeks before drinking or store for up to a year. Serve chilled.

PERRY CYSER

average abv: 8%

Do we call this one a pyser? Or maybe a cyserry? Or do we need to make up a whole new name? Whatever you choose to call it, our chimeric hybrid cider is a bubbly, fruity wonder—the quiet sweetness of the pear combined with sunny warmth of honey in one all-too-drinkable glass. Any variety of honey works well here, but I especially like it with orange-blossom, clover, or wildflower honey.

1 GALLON	INGREDIENTS	5 GALLONS
1 gal (3.8 L)	PEAR JUICE	5 gal (18.9 L)
¼ c (85 g)	HONEY, ANY VARIETY	1¼ c (425 g)
1	CAMPDEN TABLET, IF NEEDED	5
½ pkg	WHITE WINE YEAST	1 pkg
½ tsp	PECTIC ENZYME POWDER	2½ tsp
Pkg instructions	YEAST NUTRIENT	Pkg instructions
½ to 1 tsp	POWDERED ACID BLEND, IF NEEDED	2½ to 5 tsp
⅛ to ½ tsp	POWDERED WINE TANNIN, IF NEEDED	¾ to 2½ tsp
2½ Tbsp (50 g)	HONEY, ANY VARIETY, FOR BOTTLING	Scant ¾ c (250 g)
¼ c (60ml)	HOT WATER, FOR BOTTLING	1 c (240 ml)

Combine a few cups of the juice and the honey in a small saucepan. Warm over medium heat, stirring gently, until the honey has dissolved. Remove from the heat and let cool to room temperature.

Combine the honey mixture and remaining juice in a sanitized fermentation bucket. Check and record the original gravity. (If using unpasteurized juice, crush the Campden tablet[s] and whisk into the juice; snap on the lid, insert an air lock filled with sanitizer or vodka, and let the juice stand for 24 hours.)

Sprinkle the yeast, pectic enzyme, and yeast nutrient over the juice. Whisk vigorously with a sanitized whisk to dissolve the ingredients and aerate the juice. Snap on the lid and insert a filled air lock. Place the bucket out of direct sunlight and at room temperature (70° to 75°F). Fermentation should begin within 24 hours (bubbles will pop regularly through the air lock). Active fermentation will peak after a few days, and then gradually finish within 1 to 2 weeks.

Once you've seen very little activity in the air lock for a few days (a stray bubble or two is fine), siphon the cyser to a sanitized jug or carboy, leaving behind as much sediment as possible. As you transfer the cyser, taste it using a sanitized wine thief to check its progress. Insert the stopper and air lock, then place the cyser out of direct sunlight and at room temperature for another 2 weeks or up to 2 months.

When ready to bottle, taste the cyser again. If needed, add acid blend for more acidity or tannin for more astringency. Taste again a few days later, and continue adjusting and tasting until you're happy.

Check the final gravity and calculate the ABV. Dissolve the honey in the hot water and mix with the cyser, back-sweetening if desired (see page 52). Bottle the cyser. Wait 2 weeks before drinking or store for up to a year. Serve chilled.

CRISP SPARKLING CYSER

average abv: 8%

The trick to making a sparkling cyser is using enough honey to give the cyser a distinct honey flavor, but not so much that it becomes excessively boozy. Too much alcohol can inhibit the yeast activity, making it difficult to get good carbonation in the bottle. Use a darker, amber-hued variety of honey in this recipe if you can. These honeys have a stronger, more distinct flavor and give the cyser more honey character.

1 GALLON	INGREDIENTS	5 GALLONS
1 gal (3.8 L)	APPLE JUICE	5 gal (18.9 L)
¼ c (85 g)	HONEY, ANY DARK, AMBER-HUED VARIETY	1¼ c (425 g)
1	CAMPDEN TABLET, IF NEEDED	5
½ pkg	WHITE WINE YEAST	1 pkg
½ tsp	PECTIC ENZYME POWDER	2½ tsp
Pkg instructions	YEAST NUTRIENT	Pkg instructions
½ to 1 tsp	POWDERED ACID BLEND, IF NEEDED	2½ to 5 tsp
⅛ to ½ tsp	POWDERED WINE TANNIN, IF NEEDED	¾ to 2½ tsp
2½ Tbsp (50 g)	HONEY, ANY VARIETY, FOR BOTTLING	Scant ¾ c (250 g)
¼ c (60ml)	HOT WATER, FOR BOTTLING	1 c (240 ml)

Combine a few cups of the juice and the honey in a small saucepan. Warm over medium heat, stirring gently, until the honey has dissolved. Remove from the heat and let cool to room temperature.

Combine the honey mixture and remaining juice in a sanitized fermentation bucket. Check and record the original gravity. (If using unpasteurized juice, crush the Campden tablet[s] and whisk into the juice; snap on the lid, insert an air lock filled with sanitizer or vodka, and let the juice stand for 24 hours.)

Sprinkle the yeast, pectic enzyme, and yeast nutrient over the juice. Whisk vigorously with a sanitized whisk to dissolve the ingredients and aerate the juice. Snap on the lid and insert a filled air lock. Place the bucket out of direct sunlight and at room temperature (70° to 75°F). Fermentation should begin within 24 hours (bubbles will pop regularly through the air lock). Active fermentation will peak after a few days, and then gradually finish within 1 to 2 weeks.

Once you've seen very little activity in the air lock for a few days (a stray bubble or two is fine), siphon the cyser to a sanitized jug or carboy, leaving behind as much sediment as possible. As you transfer the cyser, taste it using a sanitized wine thief to check its progress. Insert the stopper and air lock, then place the cyser out of direct sunlight and at room temperature for another 2 weeks or up to 2 months.

When ready to bottle, taste the cyser again. If needed, add acid blend for more acidity or tannin for more astringency. Taste again a few days later, and continue adjusting and tasting until you're happy.

Check the final gravity and calculate the ABV. Dissolve the honey in the hot water and mix with the cyser, back-sweetening if desired (see page 52). Bottle the cyser. Wait 2 weeks before drinking or store for up to a year. Serve chilled.

modern ciders

While it's true that ciders are traditionally made from apples and apples alone, we live in modern times. This means we have access to all sorts of interesting and potentially cider-worthy ingredients. It's hard to walk through the produce section without hearing the siren call of fresh pineapples and peaches, or to pass by the baking aisle without mulling over the possibility of adding cinnamon, vanilla, and cloves to your next cider. I say embrace the times and give in to the opportunities before you.

The recipes in this chapter stretch the imagination and push the boundaries of what we know as cider. From fresh fruit to black tea to rum-infused oak cubes, they will also introduce you to all the ways that we can add flavors both bold and subtle to our homemade ciders.

BLACK AND BLUEBERRY CIDER

average abv: 6 to 8%

Start this one at the height of summer when both blackberries and blueberries are at their sweetest and ripest. Frozen berries also work well, though I find the cider tends to be more tart. If your cider ends up tart, let it go through malolactic fermentation before bottling (see page 45). I like using Montrachet wine yeast with this recipe to help bring out the deep, fruity flavors in the finished cider. Since blackberries and blueberries bring a lot of their own acids and tannins to the cider, taste carefully before adding any extra.

1 GALLON	INGREDIENTS	5 GALLONS
1 gal (3.8 L)	APPLE JUICE	5 gal (18.9 L)
1	CAMPDEN TABLET, IF NEEDED	5
½ pkg	WHITE WINE YEAST	1 pkg
½ tsp	PECTIC ENZYME POWDER	2½ tsp
Pkg instructions	YEAST NUTRIENT	Pkg instructions
2 c (340 g)	BLACKBERRIES, THAWED IF FROZEN	10 c (1.7 kg)
2 c (340 g)	BLUEBERRIES, THAWED IF FROZEN	10 c (1.7 kg)
½ to 1 tsp	POWDERED ACID BLEND, IF NEEDED	2½ to 5 tsp
⅛ to ½ tsp	POWDERED WINE TANNIN, IF NEEDED	¾ to 2½ tsp
3 Tbsp (25 g)	CORN SUGAR, FOR BOTTLING	Scant 1 c (125 g)
¼ c (60ml)	HOT WATER, FOR BOTTLING	1 c (240 ml)

Pour the juice into a sanitized fermentation bucket. Check and record the original gravity. (If using unpasteurized juice, crush the Campden tablet[s] and whisk into the juice; snap on the lid, insert an air lock filled with sanitizer or vodka, and let the juice stand for 24 hours.)

Sprinkle the yeast, pectic enzyme, and yeast nutrient over the juice. Whisk vigorously with a sanitized whisk to dissolve the ingredients and aerate the juice. Snap on

the lid and insert a filled air lock. Place the bucket out of direct sunlight and at room temperature (70° to 75°F). Fermentation should begin within 24 hours (bubbles will pop regularly through the air lock). Active fermentation will peak after a few days, and then gradually finish within 1 to 2 weeks.

Once you've seen very little activity in the air lock for a few days (a stray bubble or two is fine), place all the berries in a large mesh bag. Place the bag inside a mixing bowl, and crush the berries with a potato masher or other utensil to release their juices. Add the bag of berries and their juices to the cider, snap on the lid, and add the air lock.

Wait another 1 to 2 weeks for the cider to infuse and for any renewed fermentation to slow, then siphon the cider to a sanitized jug or carboy, leaving behind the used fruit and as much sediment as possible. As you transfer the cider, taste it using a sanitized wine thief to check its progress. Insert the stopper and air lock, then place the cider out of direct sunlight and at room temperature for another 2 weeks or up to 2 months.

When ready to bottle, taste the cider again. If needed, add acid blend for more acidity or tannin for more astringency. Taste again a few days later, and continue adjusting and tasting until you're happy.

Check the final gravity and calculate the ABV. Dissolve the corn sugar in the hot water and mix with the cider, back-sweetening if desired (see page 52). Bottle the cider. Wait 2 weeks before drinking or store for up to a year. Serve chilled.

PINEAPPLE-COCONUT CIDER

average abv: 6 to 8%

This cider is 50 percent apple juice, 50 percent pineapple juice, and 100 percent awesome. It finishes as crisp as any cider, but with a hint of sunny pineapple sweetness that lingers on the tongue. Some dried coconut added late in the game gives the cider some warm, coconut-y goodness to round everything out. Pineapple juice can be fairly tart, so it's a good match for a particularly sweet apple juice. If it still tastes overly tart toward the end, add malolactic culture to encourage a malolactic fermentation and to soften the acidity.

1 GALLON	INGREDIENTS	5 GALLONS
2 qt (1.9 L)	APPLE JUICE	2½ gal (9.5 L)
2 qt (1.9 L)	PINEAPPLE JUICE	2½ gal (9.5 L)
1	CAMPDEN TABLET, IF NEEDED	5
½ pkg	WHITE WINE YEAST	1 pkg
½ tsp	PECTIC ENZYME POWDER	2½ tsp
Pkg instructions	YEAST NUTRIENT	Pkg instructions
½ c (42 g)	UNSWEETENED COCONUT FLAKES	2½ c (212 g)
½ to 1 tsp	POWDERED ACID BLEND, IF NEEDED	2½ to 5 tsp
⅛ to ½ tsp	POWDERED WINE TANNIN, IF NEEDED	¾ to 2½ tsp
3 Tbsp (25 g)	CORN SUGAR, FOR BOTTLING	Scant 1 c (125 g)
¼ c (60ml)	HOT WATER, FOR BOTTLING	1 c (240 ml)

Pour the juices into a sanitized fermentation bucket. Check and record the original gravity. (If using unpasteurized juice, crush the Campden tablet[s] and whisk into the juice; snap on the lid, insert an air lock filled with sanitizer or vodka, and let the juice stand for 24 hours.)

Sprinkle the yeast, pectic enzyme, and yeast nutrient over the juice. Whisk vigorously with a sanitized whisk to dissolve the ingredients and aerate the juice. Snap on the lid and insert a filled air lock. Place the bucket out of direct sunlight and at room temperature (70° to 75°F). Fermentation should begin within 24 hours (bubbles will pop regularly through the air lock). Active fermentation will peak after a few days, and then gradually finish within 1 to 2 weeks.

Once you've seen very little activity in the air lock for a few days (a stray bubble or two is fine), measure the coconut into a mesh bag and place in a sanitized jug or carboy. Siphon the cider over the top, leaving behind as much sediment as possible. As you transfer the cider, taste it with a sanitized wine thief to check its progress. Insert the stopper and air lock, then place the cider out of direct sunlight and at room temperature for another 2 weeks or up to 2 months. Taste regularly and remove the coconut when you like the flavor (you can also add more coconut for stronger flavor, if you'd like).

When ready to bottle, taste the cider again. If needed, add acid blend for more acidity or tannin for more astringency. Taste again a few days later, and continue adjusting and tasting until you're happy.

Check the final gravity and calculate the ABV. Dissolve the corn sugar in the hot water and mix with the cider, back-sweetening if desired (see page 52). Bottle the cider. Wait 2 weeks before drinking or store for up to a year. Serve chilled.

SMOKY BBQ APPLE-PEAR CIDER

average abv: 6 to 8%

This recipe uses a rather unexpected ingredient: a smoked tea called Lapsang Souchong, which you can find through most tea sellers or online. This tea adds all the smoky goodness you could hope for in a cider, without the need to purchase a smoker. (If you have a smoker, by all means smoke your apples before pressing them. And then send me a bottle, *pleaseandthankyou!*) The tea's smoky flavor can quickly overwhelm the cider, so start with the amount listed and add more after a few days if you think the cider needs it.

1 GALLON	INGREDIENTS	5 GALLONS
2 qt (1.9 L)	APPLE JUICE	2½ gal (9.5 L)
2 qt (1.9 L)	PEAR JUICE	2½ gal (9.5 L)
1	CAMPDEN TABLET, IF NEEDED	5
½ pkg	WHITE WINE YEAST	1 pkg
½ tsp	PECTIC ENZYME POWDER	2½ tsp
Pkg instructions	YEAST NUTRIENT	Pkg instructions
2 tsp	LAPSANG SOUCHONG BLACK TEA	3 Tbsp
½ to 1 tsp	POWDERED ACID BLEND, IF NEEDED	2½ to 5 tsp
⅛ to ½ tsp	POWDERED WINE TANNIN, IF NEEDED	¾ to 2½ tsp
3 Tbsp (25 g)	CORN SUGAR, FOR BOTTLING	Scant 1 c (125 g)
¼ c (60ml)	HOT WATER, FOR BOTTLING	1 c (240 ml)

Pour the juices into a sanitized fermentation bucket. Check and record the original gravity. (If using unpasteurized juice, crush the Campden tablet[s] and whisk into the juice; snap on the lid, insert an air lock filled with sanitizer or vodka, and let the juice stand for 24 hours.)

Sprinkle the yeast, pectic enzyme, and yeast nutrient over the juice. Whisk vigorously with a sanitized whisk to dissolve the ingredients and aerate the juice. Snap on the lid and insert a filled air lock. Place the bucket out of direct sunlight and at room temperature (70° to 75°F). Fermentation should begin within 24 hours (bubbles will pop regularly through the air lock). Active fermentation will peak after a few days, and then gradually finish within 1 to 2 weeks.

Once you've seen very little activity in the air lock for a few days (a stray bubble or two is fine), measure the tea into a mesh bag and place in a sanitized jug or carboy. Siphon the cider over the top, leaving behind as much sediment as possible. As you transfer the cider, taste it using a sanitized wine thief to check its progress. Insert the stopper and air lock, then place the cider out of direct sunlight and at room temperature for another 2 weeks or up to 2 months. Taste regularly and remove the tea when you like the flavor.

When ready to bottle, taste the cider again. If needed, add acid blend for more acidity or tannin for more astringency. Taste again a few days later, and continue adjusting and tasting until you're happy.

Check the final gravity and calculate the ABV. Dissolve the corn sugar in the hot water and mix with the cider, back-sweetening if desired (see page 52). Bottle the cider. Wait 2 weeks before drinking or store for up to a year. Serve chilled.

CHERRY-POMEGRANATE CIDER

average abv: 6 to 8%

This cider is a perfect example of maximum reward for minimal effort. Just use store-bought cherry juice and pomegranate juice, and mix them into the apple juice base—so much easier than juicing your own fruit. Be sure to buy 100 percent pure fruit juice for this; it's more expensive than juice from concentrate, but the final flavor will be well worth the extra pennies. Pomegranate juice has a lot of tannin, so taste the cider carefully before adding any extra.

1 GALLON	INGREDIENTS	5 GALLONS
3 qt (2.8 L)	APPLE JUICE	3¾ gal (14.2 L)
3 c (0.7 L)	CHERRY JUICE	15 c (3.5 L)
1 c (240ml)	POMEGRANATE JUICE	5 c (1.2 L)
1	CAMPDEN TABLET, IF NEEDED	5
½ pkg	WHITE WINE YEAST	1 pkg
½ tsp	PECTIC ENZYME POWDER	2½ tsp
Pkg instructions	YEAST NUTRIENT	Pkg instructions
½ to 1 tsp	POWDERED ACID BLEND, IF NEEDED	2½ to 5 tsp
⅛ to ½ tsp	POWDERED WINE TANNIN, IF NEEDED	¾ to 2½ tsp
3 Tbsp (25 g)	CORN SUGAR, FOR BOTTLING	Scant 1 c (125 g)
¼ c (60ml)	HOT WATER, FOR BOTTLING	1 c (240 ml)

Pour the juices into a sanitized fermentation bucket. Check and record the original gravity. (If using unpasteurized juice, crush the Campden tablet[s] and whisk into the juice; snap on the lid, insert an air lock filled with sanitizer or vodka, and let the juice stand for 24 hours.)

Sprinkle the yeast, pectic enzyme, and yeast nutrient over the juice. Whisk vigorously with a sanitized whisk to dissolve the ingredients and aerate the juice. Snap on the lid and insert a filled air lock. Place the bucket out of direct sunlight and at room temperature (70° to 75°F). Fermentation should begin within 24 hours (bubbles will pop regularly through the air lock). Active fermentation will peak after a few days, and then gradually finish within 1 to 2 weeks.

Once you've seen very little activity in the air lock for a few days (a stray bubble or two is fine), siphon the cider to a sanitized jug or carboy, leaving behind as much sediment as possible. As you transfer the cider, taste it using a sanitized wine thief to check its progress. Insert the stopper and air lock, then place the cider out of direct sunlight and at room temperature for another 2 weeks or up to 2 months.

When ready to bottle, taste the cider again. If needed, add acid blend for more acidity or tannin for more astringency. Taste again a few days later, and continue adjusting and tasting until you're happy.

Check the final gravity and calculate the ABV. Dissolve the corn sugar in the hot water and mix with the cider, back-sweetening if desired (see page 52). Bottle the cider. Wait 2 weeks before drinking or store for up to a year. Serve chilled.

SPICED WINTER CIDER

average abv: 6 to 8%

Cinnamon and clove give this cider a soft, spicy flavor, and the addition of orange adds a warm, citrusy note that's perfect for the holidays. Use a vegetable peeler to strip long pieces of zest from the orange, leaving as much bitter white pith behind as possible. Also, taste the cider often once you add the spices, and either bottle or remove the spices once the flavor of the cider suits your taste.

1 GALLON	INGREDIENTS	5 GALLONS
1 gal (3.8 L)	APPLE JUICE	5 gal (18.9 L)
1	CAMPDEN TABLET, IF NEEDED	5
½ pkg	ENGLISH ALE OR CIDER YEAST	1 pkg
½ tsp	PECTIC ENZYME POWDER	2½ tsp
Pkg instructions	YEAST NUTRIENT	Pkg instructions
1	WHOLE 3-INCH CINNAMON STICK	4
1	WHOLE CLOVE	3
½ tsp	WHOLE BLACK PEPPERCORNS	2 tsp
From 1 medium orange	ORANGE ZEST	From 4 medium oranges
½ to 1 tsp	POWDERED ACID BLEND, IF NEEDED	2½ to 5 tsp
⅛ to ½ tsp	POWDERED WINE TANNIN, IF NEEDED	¾ to 2½ tsp
2½ Tbsp (50 g)	HONEY, ANY VARIETY, FOR BOTTLING	Scant ¾ c (250 g)
¼ c (60ml)	HOT WATER, FOR BOTTLING	1 c (240 ml)

Pour the juice into a sanitized fermentation bucket. Check and record the original gravity. (If using unpasteurized juice, crush the Campden tablet[s] and whisk into the juice; snap on the lid, insert an air lock filled with sanitizer or vodka, and let the juice stand for 24 hours.)

Sprinkle the yeast, pectic enzyme, and yeast nutrient over the juice. Whisk vigorously with a sanitized whisk to dissolve the ingredients and aerate the juice. Snap on the lid and insert a filled air lock. Place the bucket out of direct sunlight and at room temperature (70° to 75°F). Fermentation should begin within 24 hours (bubbles will pop regularly through the air lock). Active fermentation will peak after a few days, and then gradually finish within 1 to 2 weeks.

Once you've seen very little activity in the air lock for a few days (a stray bubble or two is fine), measure the spices and orange zest into a mesh bag and place in a sanitized jug or carboy. Siphon the cider over the top, leaving behind as much sediment as possible. As you transfer the cider, taste it using a sanitized wine thief to check its progress. Insert the stopper and air lock, then place the cider out of direct sunlight and at room temperature for another 2 weeks or up to 2 months. Taste regularly and remove the spices when you like the flavor.

When ready to bottle, taste the cider again. If needed, add acid blend for more acidity or tannin for more astringency. Taste again a few days later, and continue adjusting and tasting until you're happy.

Check the final gravity and calculate the ABV. Dissolve the honey in the hot water and mix with the cider, back-sweetening if desired (see page 52). Bottle the cider. Wait 2 weeks before drinking or store for up to a year. Serve chilled.

RUBY RED GRAPEFRUIT CIDER

average abv: 6 to 8%

Citrus fruit and cider make such a good pairing—something I wouldn't have guessed before trying it myself. This grapefruit cider could rival any IPA for its bitter, citrusy goodness, no hops needed. You only need the grapefruit zest for this recipe—no juice or citrus-flavored baking extracts. Use a vegetable peeler to strip away long pieces of the zest, leaving behind as much of the bitter white pith as possible.

1 GALLON	INGREDIENTS	5 GALLONS
1 gal (3.8 L)	APPLE JUICE	5 gal (18.9 L)
1	CAMPDEN TABLET, IF NEEDED	5
½ pkg	WHITE WINE YEAST	1 pkg
½ tsp	PECTIC ENZYME POWDER	2½ tsp
Pkg instructions	YEAST NUTRIENT	Pkg instructions
From ½ large grapefruit	RUBY RED GRAPEFRUIT ZEST	From 2½ large grapefruit
½ to 1 tsp	POWDERED ACID BLEND, IF NEEDED	2½ to 5 tsp
⅛ to ½ tsp	POWDERED WINE TANNIN, IF NEEDED	¾ to 2½ tsp
3 Tbsp (25 g)	CORN SUGAR, FOR BOTTLING	Scant 1 c (125 g)
¼ c (60ml)	HOT WATER, FOR BOTTLING	1 c (240 ml)

Pour the juice into a sanitized fermentation bucket. Check and record the original gravity. (If using unpasteurized juice, crush the Campden tablet[s] and whisk into the juice; snap on the lid, insert an air lock filled with sanitizer or vodka, and let the juice stand for 24 hours.)

Sprinkle the yeast, pectic enzyme, and yeast nutrient over the juice. Whisk vigorously with a sanitized whisk to dissolve the ingredients and aerate the juice. Snap on the lid and insert a filled air lock. Place the bucket out of direct sunlight and at room temperature (70° to 75°F).

Fermentation should begin within 24 hours (bubbles will pop regularly through the air lock). Active fermentation will peak after a few days, and then gradually finish within 1 to 2 weeks.

Once you've seen very little activity in the air lock for a few days (a stray bubble or two is fine), measure the zest into a mesh bag and place in a sanitized jug or carboy. Siphon the cider over the top, leaving behind as much sediment as possible. As you transfer the cider, taste it using a sanitized wine thief to check its progress. Insert the stopper and air lock, then place the cider out of direct sunlight and at room temperature for another 2 weeks or up to 2 months. Taste regularly and remove the zest when you like the flavor.

When ready to bottle, taste the cider again. If needed, add acid blend for more acidity or tannin for more astringency. Taste again a few days later, and continue adjusting and tasting until you're happy.

Check the final gravity and calculate the ABV. Dissolve the corn sugar in the hot water and mix with the cider, back-sweetening if desired (see page 52). Bottle the cider. Wait 2 weeks before drinking or store for up to a year. Serve chilled.

CIDER DE JAMAICA (HIBISCUS CIDER)

average abv: 6 to 8%

Since moving to California with its wealth of taquerias, I have learned that there is no better companion to a plate of spicy tacos than an ice-cold glass of agua de jamaica. This is an iced tea made from dried hibiscus flowers that is often flavored with cinnamon, ginger, and a squeeze of lime. The drink is simultaneously sweet, tart, and floral. Of course, I had to make my own "cider de jamaica" for Taco Tuesdays at home. Add the squeeze of lime to each glass as you serve.

1 GALLON	INGREDIENTS	5 GALLONS
1 gal (3.8 L)	APPLE JUICE	5 gal (18.9 L)
1	CAMPDEN TABLET, IF NEEDED	5
½ pkg	WHITE WINE YEAST	1 pkg
½ tsp	PECTIC ENZYME POWDER	2½ tsp
Pkg instructions	YEAST NUTRIENT	Pkg instructions
1 c (60 g)	DRIED HIBISCUS FLOWERS	5 c (300 g)
1	WHOLE 3-INCH CINNAMON STICK (OPTIONAL)	4
1-inch piece (15 g)	FRESH GINGER, GRATED (OPTIONAL)	4-inch piece (60 g)
½ to 1 tsp	POWDERED ACID BLEND, IF NEEDED	2½ to 5 tsp
⅛ to ½ tsp	POWDERED WINE TANNIN, IF NEEDED	¾ to 2½ tsp
3 Tbsp (25 g)	CORN SUGAR, FOR BOTTLING	Scant 1 c (125 g)
¼ c (60ml)	HOT WATER, FOR BOTTLING	1 c (240 ml)

Pour the juice into a sanitized fermentation bucket. Check and record the original gravity. (If using unpasteurized juice, crush the Campden tablet[s] and whisk into the juice; snap on the lid, insert an air lock filled with sanitizer or vodka, and let the juice stand for 24 hours.)

Sprinkle the yeast, pectic enzyme, and yeast nutrient over the juice. Whisk vigorously with a sanitized whisk to dissolve the ingredients and aerate the juice. Snap on the lid and insert a filled air lock. Place the bucket out of direct sunlight and at room temperature (70° to 75°F). Fermentation should begin within 24 hours (bubbles will pop regularly through the air lock). Active fermentation will peak after a few days, and then gradually finish within 1 to 2 weeks.

Once you've seen very little activity in the air lock for a few days (a stray bubble or two is fine), measure the hibiscus flowers, cinnamon, and ginger(if using) into a mesh bag and place in a sanitized jug or carboy. Siphon the cider over the top, leaving behind as much sediment as possible. As you transfer the cider, taste it using a sanitized wine thief to check its progress. Insert the stopper and air lock, then place the cider out of direct sunlight and at room temperature for another 2 weeks or up to 2 months. Taste regularly and remove the flowers and spices when you like the flavor (you can also add more flowers or spices for stronger flavor, if you'd like).

When ready to bottle, taste the cider again. If needed, add acid blend for more acidity or tannin for more astringency. Taste again a few days later, and continue adjusting and tasting until you're happy.

Check the final gravity and calculate the ABV. Dissolve the corn sugar in the hot water and mix with the cider, back-sweetening if desired (see page 52). Bottle the cider. Wait 2 weeks before drinking or store for up to a year. Refrigerate before drinking.

DARK AND STORMY CIDER

average abv: 8.5%

For me, Dark and Stormy cocktails are forever linked with beach vacations and long, luxurious afternoons spent doing nothing but reading dog-eared paperbacks on deck chairs. For this cider-based riff, I infuse the cider with fresh ginger and rum-soaked oak cubes to mimic the flavors of the original drink. Bottle it up, pack it in your cooler, and you've got a beach-worthy cocktail all ready to go. The potency of fresh ginger can really vary, so start with the amount here and add more if it's not strong enough for your taste.

1 GALLON	INGREDIENTS	5 GALLONS
1 gal (3.8 L)	APPLE JUICE	5 gal (18.9 L)
1	CAMPDEN TABLET, IF NEEDED	5
½ pkg	ENGLISH ALE OR CIDER YEAST	1 pkg
½ tsp	PECTIC ENZYME POWDER	2½ tsp
Pkg instructions	YEAST NUTRIENT	Pkg instructions
½ oz (15 g)	OAK CUBES	2½ oz (70 g)
¼ c (60 ml)	DARK RUM	1¼ c (300 ml)
1 (30 g)	FRESH GINGER, 2-INCH PIECE	5 (150 g)
½ to 1 tsp	POWDERED ACID BLEND, IF NEEDED	2½ to 5 tsp
⅛ to ½ tsp	POWDERED WINE TANNIN, IF NEEDED	¾ to 2½ tsp
3 Tbsp (25 g)	CORN SUGAR, FOR BOTTLING	Scant 1 c (125 g)
¼ c (60ml)	HOT WATER, FOR BOTTLING	1 c (240 ml)

Pour the juice into a sanitized fermentation bucket. Check and record the original gravity. (If using unpasteurized juice, crush the Campden tablet[s] and whisk into the juice; snap on the lid, insert an air lock filled with sanitizer or vodka, and let the juice stand for 24 hours.)

Sprinkle the yeast, pectic enzyme, and yeast nutrient over the juice. Whisk vigorously with a sanitized whisk to dissolve the ingredients and aerate the juice. Snap on the lid and insert a filled air lock. Place the bucket out of direct sunlight and at room temperature (70° to 75°F). Fermentation should begin within 24 hours (bubbles will pop regularly through the air lock). Active fermentation will peak after a few days, and then gradually finish within 1 to 2 weeks.

Meanwhile, combine the oak cubes and rum in a small container. Soak for at least 1 week, or until the cider has finished actively fermenting.

Once you've seen very little activity in the air lock for a few days (a stray bubble or two is fine), peel and grate the ginger using a Microplane or the small holes on a box grater. Strain the oak cubes from the rum, reserving the rum. Measure the ginger and oak cubes into a mesh bag and place in a sanitized jug or carboy. Siphon the cider over the top, leaving behind as much sediment as possible. As you transfer the cider, taste it using a sanitized wine thief to check its progress. Insert the stopper and air lock, then place the cider out of direct sunlight and at room temperature for another 2 weeks or up to 2 months. Taste regularly and remove the ginger and oak cubes when you like the flavor (you can also add the reserved rum for stronger flavor, if you'd like).

When ready to bottle, taste the cider again. If needed, add acid blend for more acidity or tannin for more astringency. Taste again a few days later, and continue adjusting and tasting until you're happy.

Check the final gravity and calculate the ABV. Dissolve the corn sugar in the hot water and mix with the cider, back-sweetening if desired (see page 52). Bottle the cider. Wait 2 weeks before drinking or store for up to a year. Serve chilled.

ciders for beer lovers

Before I was a cider maker, I was a beer brewer, so it was really only a matter of time before I started experimenting with cider-based riffs on some of my favorite brews. I call these "beer-kissed ciders"—they are still definitely ciders, but they are imbued with some of the character, flavor, and spirit of classic beers.

There are two ways to give your ciders a little of this beer spirit. First, use a strain of beer yeast most associated with the beer style, like a California yeast for an IPA-style cider or a Belgian yeast for a saison-style cider. Yeast plays a big role in the flavor of a finished beer, and it can here, as well. If you need to make sure your cider is totally gluten-free, just remember to double-check that the yeast you are using is also gluten-free.

Second, use hops, spices, fruit, and other flavorful pantry ingredients to infuse the cider and mimic the flavors of different beer styles. You often hear beers described with words like "fruity," "herbal," and "citrusy." When making a beer-kissed cider, just turn those descriptors into reality, and use real fruit, fresh herbs, and citrus zest to bring those flavors into the cider.

There is only so far you can push a cider into beer territory. It would be difficult to make a porter-style cider or a doppelbock-style cider, for instance. This said, I'm all for experimentation, and I give you every encouragement in the pursuit of your beer-kissed cider dreams!

DRY-HOPPED WEST COAST IPC:
INDIA PALE CIDER

average abv: 6 to 8%

In the beer world, a hoppy IPA (India pale ale) usually means a bitter, tongue-twisting brew. Hoppy ciders are something different. They are more delicate and far less bitter, with flavors and aromas ranging from herbal to woodsy to bright citrus. An IPC is made by infusing the cider with a dose of hops before bottling, called "dry hopping." (To any beer brewers who might be thinking of giving your cider a full hop boil, I'd advise against it. In my experiments, a hop boil resulted in an unpleasant cooked apple flavor and negligible bitterness. However, a quick boil of 5 to 10 minutes does add some extra hop flavor, if you'd like.)

1 GALLON	INGREDIENTS	5 GALLONS
1 gal (3.8 L)	APPLE JUICE	5 gal (18.9 L)
1	CAMPDEN TABLET, IF NEEDED	5
½ pkg	CALIFORNIA ALE YEAST	1 pkg
½ tsp	PECTIC ENZYME POWDER	2½ tsp
Pkg instructions	YEAST NUTRIENT	Pkg instructions
⅓ oz (10 g)	CHINOOK PELLET HOPS (12% AA)	1¾ oz (50 g)
½ to 1 tsp	POWDERED ACID BLEND, IF NEEDED	2½ to 5 tsp
⅛ to ½ tsp	POWDERED WINE TANNIN, IF NEEDED	¾ to 2½ tsp
3 Tbsp (25 g)	CORN SUGAR, FOR BOTTLING	Scant 1 c (125 g)
¼ c (60ml)	HOT WATER, FOR BOTTLING	1 c (240 ml)

Pour the juice into a sanitized fermentation bucket. Check and record the original gravity. (If using unpasteurized juice, crush the Campden tablet[s] and whisk into the juice; snap on the lid, insert an air lock filled with sanitizer or vodka, and let the juice stand for 24 hours.)

Sprinkle the yeast, pectic enzyme, and yeast nutrient over the juice. Whisk vigorously with a sanitized whisk to dissolve the ingredients and aerate the juice. Snap on the lid and insert a filled air lock. Place the bucket out of direct sunlight and at room temperature (70° to 75°F). Fermentation should begin within 24 hours (bubbles will pop regularly through the air lock). Active fermentation will peak after a few days, and then gradually finish within 1 to 2 weeks.

Once you've seen very little activity in the air lock for a few days (a stray bubble or two is fine), measure the hops into a mesh bag and place in a sanitized jug or carboy. Siphon the cider over the top, leaving behind as much sediment as possible. As you transfer the cider, taste it using a sanitized wine thief to check its progress. Insert the stopper and air lock, then place the cider out of direct sunlight and at room temperature for another 2 weeks or up to 2 months. Taste regularly and remove the hops when you like the flavor.

When ready to bottle, taste the cider again. If needed, add acid blend for more acidity or tannin for more astringency. Taste again a few days later, and continue adjusting and tasting until you're happy.

Check the final gravity and calculate the ABV. Dissolve the corn sugar in the hot water and mix with the cider, back-sweetening if desired (see page 52). Bottle the cider. Wait 2 weeks before drinking or store for up to a year. Serve chilled.

DRY-HOPPED ENGLISH ESC: EXTRA-SPECIAL CIDER

average abv: 6 to 8%

A British extra-special bitter (ESB) is a malty ale balanced by a smattering of earthy and herbal hops. My secret weapon for adding "maltiness" to a cider is dark or amber-hued honey. I like buckwheat honey for its nutty, caramel-like flavor. Dry-hop with some English hops, and our cider simulacrum is complete.

1 GALLON	INGREDIENTS	5 GALLONS
2 qt (1.9 L)	APPLE JUICE	2½ gal (9.5 L)
2 qt (1.9 L)	PEAR JUICE	2½ gal (9.5 L)
¼ c (85 g)	BUCKWHEAT HONEY OR OTHER DARK, AMBER-HUED HONEY	1¼ c (425 g)
1	CAMPDEN TABLET, IF NEEDED	5
½ pkg	ENGLISH ALE YEAST	1 pkg
½ tsp	PECTIC ENZYME POWDER	2½ tsp
Pkg instructions	YEAST NUTRIENT	Pkg instructions
½ oz (14 g)	FUGGLE PELLET HOPS (4% AA)	2½ oz (70 g)
½ to 1 tsp	POWDERED ACID BLEND, IF NEEDED	2½ to 5 tsp
⅛ to ½ tsp	POWDERED WINE TANNIN, IF NEEDED	¾ to 2½ tsp
2½ Tbsp (50 g)	HONEY, ANY VARIETY, FOR BOTTLING	Scant ¾ c (250 g)
¼ c (60ml)	HOT WATER, FOR BOTTLING	1 c (240 ml)

Combine a few cups of the juices and the honey in a small saucepan. Warm over medium heat, stirring gently, until the honey has dissolved. Remove from the heat and let cool to room temperature.

Combine the honey mixture and remaining juice in a sanitized fermentation bucket. Check and record the original gravity. (If using unpasteurized juice, crush the Campden tablet[s] and whisk into the juice; snap on the lid, insert an air lock filled with sanitizer or vodka, and let the juice stand for 24 hours.)

Sprinkle the yeast, pectic enzyme, and yeast nutrient over the juice. Whisk vigorously with a sanitized whisk to dissolve the ingredients and aerate the juice. Snap on the lid and insert a filled air lock. Place the bucket out of direct sunlight and at room temperature (70° to 75°F). Fermentation should begin within 24 hours (bubbles will pop regularly through the air lock). Active fermentation will peak after a few days, and then gradually finish within 1 to 2 weeks.

Once you've seen very little activity in the air lock for a few days (a stray bubble or two is fine), measure the hops into a mesh bag and place in a sanitized jug or carboy. Siphon the cider over the top, leaving behind as much sediment as possible. As you transfer the cider, taste it using a sanitized wine thief to check its progress. Insert the stopper and air lock, then place the cider out of direct sunlight and at room temperature for another 2 weeks or up to 2 months. Taste regularly and remove the hops when you like the flavor.

When ready to bottle, taste the cider again. If needed, add acid blend for more acidity or tannin for more astringency. Taste again a few days later, and continue adjusting and tasting until you're happy.

Check the final gravity and calculate the ABV. Dissolve the honey in the hot water and mix with the cider, back-sweetening if desired (see page 52). Bottle the cider. Wait 2 weeks before drinking or store for up to a year. Serve chilled.

BELGIAN TRAPPIST-STYLE CIDER

average abv: 6 to 8%

Belgian beers are a fruity bunch. This cider is a nod to the fruitiest of the fruity: the Belgian quadruple. This beer is typified by the flavors of dried plum, fig, cherry, and raisin, which make an easy jump into cider territory. Use dried fruit here instead of fresh because they give the cider a little extra sweetness and body. Also, simmering the fruit with a little apple juice and then letting the fruit go through the first stage of active fermentation results in a more unified fruity flavor, which is desirable for this style.

1 GALLON	INGREDIENTS	5 GALLONS
½ c (85 g)	MIXED DRIED FIGS, CHERRIES, PLUMS, AND RAISINS (PACKED)	2½ c (425 g)
1 gal (3.8 L)	APPLE JUICE	5 gal (18.9 L)
1	CAMPDEN TABLET, IF NEEDED	5
½ pkg	BELGIAN ALE YEAST	1 pkg
½ tsp	PECTIC ENZYME POWDER	2½ tsp
Pkg instructions	YEAST NUTRIENT	Pkg instructions
½ to 1 tsp	POWDERED ACID BLEND, IF NEEDED	2½ to 5 tsp
⅛ to ½ tsp	POWDERED WINE TANNIN, IF NEEDED	¾ to 2½ tsp
3 Tbsp (25 g)	CORN SUGAR, FOR BOTTLING	Scant 1 c (125 g)
¼ c (60ml)	HOT WATER, FOR BOTTLING	1 c (240 ml)

Place the dried fruit in a small saucepan and cover with some of the apple juice by about an inch. Bring to a rapid simmer over medium-high heat, and simmer for about 5 minutes. Remove the pan from the heat and let cool to room temperature.

Combine the dried fruit mixture and remaining juice in a sanitized fermentation bucket. Check and record the original gravity. (If using unpasteurized juice, crush the Campden tablet[s] and whisk into the juice; snap on the lid, insert an air lock filled with sanitizer or vodka, and let the juice stand for 24 hours.)

Sprinkle the yeast, pectic enzyme, and yeast nutrient over the juice. Whisk vigorously with a sanitized whisk to dissolve the ingredients and aerate the juice. Snap on the lid and insert a filled air lock. Place the bucket out of direct sunlight and at room temperature (70° to 75°F). Fermentation should begin within 24 hours, (bubbles will pop regularly through the air lock). Active fermentation will peak after a few days, and then gradually finish within 1 to 2 weeks.

Once you've seen very little activity in the air lock for a few days (a stray bubble or two is fine), siphon the cider to a sanitized jug or carboy, leaving behind the dried fruit and as much sediment as possible. As you transfer the cider, taste it using a sanitized wine thief to check its progress. Insert the stopper and air lock, then place the cider out of direct sunlight and at room temperature for another 2 weeks or up to 2 months.

When ready to bottle, taste the cider again. If needed, add acid blend for more acidity or tannin for more astringency. Taste again a few days later, and continue adjusting and tasting until you're happy.

Check the final gravity and calculate the ABV. Dissolve the corn sugar in the hot water and mix with the cider, back-sweetening if desired (see page 52). Bottle the cider. Wait 2 weeks before drinking or store for up to a year. Serve chilled.

BELGIAN WIT-PERRY

average abv: 6 to 8%

I have yet to meet a witbier I didn't like, and that includes this perry-based version. It's slightly sweet, a touch tangy, and infused with the traditional witbier flavors of dried bitter orange peel and coriander. Traditional witbiers are also so hazy in the glass that they almost glow with an inner light, so you can skip the pectic enzyme with this batch. Look for bitter orange peel on your next trip to the homebrew store; you're not likely to find it elsewhere.

1 GALLON	INGREDIENTS	5 GALLONS
3 qt (2.8 L)	PEAR JUICE	3¾ gal (14.2 L)
1 qt (0.9 L)	APPLE JUICE	1¼ gal (4.7 L)
1	CAMPDEN TABLET, IF NEEDED	5
½ pkg	BELGIAN WIT OR ALE YEAST	1 pkg
Pkg instructions	YEAST NUTRIENT	Pkg instructions
1½ tsp	WHOLE CORIANDER SEED	2½ Tbsp
⅙ oz (4 g)	HALLERTAUER PELLET HOPS (4% AA)	¾ oz (20 g)
¼ oz (7 g)	DRIED BITTER ORANGE PEEL	1¼ oz (35 g)
½ to 1 tsp	POWDERED ACID BLEND, IF NEEDED	2½ to 5 tsp
⅛ to ½ tsp	POWDERED WINE TANNIN, IF NEEDED	¾ to 2½ tsp
3 Tbsp (25 g)	CORN SUGAR, FOR BOTTLING	Scant 1 c (125 g)
¼ c (60ml)	HOT WATER, FOR BOTTLING	1 c (240 ml)

Pour the juices into a sanitized fermentation bucket. Check and record the original gravity. (If using unpasteurized juice, crush the Campden tablet[s] and whisk into the juice; snap on the lid, insert an air lock filled with sanitizer or vodka, and let the juice stand for 24 hours.)

Sprinkle the yeast and yeast nutrient over the juice. Whisk vigorously with a sanitized whisk to dissolve the ingredients and aerate the juice. Snap on the lid and insert a filled air lock. Place the bucket out of direct sunlight and at room temperature (70° to 75°F). Fermentation should begin within 24 hours (bubbles will pop regularly through the air lock). Active fermentation will peak after a few days, and then gradually finish within 1 to 2 weeks.

Once you've seen very little activity in the air lock for a few days (a stray bubble or two is fine), coarsely grind the coriander using a spice grinder. Transfer the coriander seed, hops, and bitter orange peel to a mesh bag and place in a sanitized jug or carboy. Siphon the perry over the top, leaving behind as much sediment as possible. As you transfer the perry, taste it using a sanitized wine thief to check its progress. Insert the stopper and air lock, then place the perry out of direct sunlight and at room temperature for another 2 weeks or up to 2 months. Taste regularly and remove the spices and hops when you like the flavor.

When ready to bottle, taste the perry again. If needed, add acid blend for more acidity or tannin for more astringency. Taste again a few days later, and continue adjusting and tasting until you're happy.

Check the final gravity and calculate the ABV. Dissolve the corn sugar in the hot water and mix with the perry, back-sweetening if desired (see page 52). Bottle the perry. Wait 2 weeks before drinking or store for up to a year. Serve chilled.

BERLINER CIDER-WEISSE

average abv: 6 to 8%

Berliner weisse beers have a flavor like sour candies. They flood your whole mouth with an intense punch before rushing away into a crisp, clean finish. Very addictive. In both the beer and our cider version, this sour flavor comes from a *Lactobacillus* culture added at the start of fermentation. This is the same bacteria responsible for the tangy flavor of yogurt, sourdough bread, and sauerkraut, so you can imagine its impact here! I've left this particular recipe fairly simple, flavored with just a hint of hops, but I've also made some excellent versions with fresh fruit (try peaches or raspberries). Also, if you can't find Ahtanum hops, any citrusy or fruity hop will do.

1 GALLON	INGREDIENTS	5 GALLONS
1 gal (3.8 L)	APPLE JUICE	5 gal (18.9 L)
1	CAMPDEN TABLET, IF NEEDED	5
½ pkg	WHEAT BEER YEAST	1 pkg
½ pkg	LACTOBACILLUS CULTURE	1 pkg
½ tsp	PECTIC ENZYME POWDER	2½ tsp
Pkg instructions	YEAST NUTRIENT	Pkg instructions
¹⁄₁₀ oz (3 g)	AHTANUM PELLET HOPS (6% AA)	½ oz (15 g)
½ to 1 tsp	POWDERED ACID BLEND, IF NEEDED	2½ to 5 tsp
⅛ to ½ tsp	POWDERED WINE TANNIN, IF NEEDED	¾ to 2½ tsp
3 Tbsp (25 g)	CORN SUGAR, FOR BOTTLING	Scant 1 c (125 g)
¼ c (60ml)	HOT WATER, FOR BOTTLING	1 c (240 ml)

Pour the juice into a sanitized fermentation bucket. Check and record the original gravity. (If using unpasteurized juice, crush the Campden tablet[s] and whisk into the juice; snap on the lid, insert an air lock filled with sanitizer or vodka, and let the juice stand for 24 hours.)

Sprinkle the yeast, *Lactobacillus*, pectic enzyme, and yeast nutrient over the juice. Whisk vigorously with a sanitized whisk to dissolve the ingredients and aerate the juice. Snap on the lid and insert a filled air lock. Place the bucket out of direct sunlight and at room temperature (70° to 75°F). Fermentation should begin within 24 hours (bubbles will pop regularly through the air lock). Active fermentation will peak after a few days, and then gradually finish within 1 to 2 weeks.

Once you've seen very little activity in the air lock for a few days (a stray bubble or two is fine), measure the hops into a mesh bag and place in a sanitized jug or carboy. Siphon the cider over the top, leaving behind as much sediment as possible. As you transfer the cider, taste it using a sanitized wine thief to check its progress. Insert the stopper and air lock, then place the cider out of direct sunlight and at room temperature for another 2 weeks or up to 2 months. Taste regularly and remove the hops when you like the flavor.

When ready to bottle, taste the cider again. If needed, add acid blend for more acidity or tannin for more astringency. Taste again a few days later, and continue adjusting and tasting until you're happy.

Check the final gravity and calculate the ABV. Dissolve the corn sugar in the hot water and mix with the cider, back-sweetening if desired (see page 52). Bottle the cider. Wait 2 weeks before drinking or store for up to a year. Serve chilled.

BOURBON BARREL–AGED CIDER
average abv: 9%

Since most of us don't have random bourbon barrels lying around our homes, we make a "barrel-aged" cider by adding toasted oak cubes soaked in bourbon to the cider before bottling. These cubes are sold at homebrewing and winemaking stores, and they'll give your cider the warm, toasted, oaky flavor that you're after. Taste the cider regularly after adding the cubes and remove them as soon as you like the flavor; leaving them for too long can give your cider an unpleasant woody flavor like wet pencil shavings. I also add boiled cider to give the finished cider a more robust apple flavor; you can purchase this ingredient online or make it yourself by boiling a gallon of apple juice into a concentrated syrup.

1 GALLON	INGREDIENTS	5 GALLONS
1 gal (3.8 L)	APPLE JUICE	5 gal (18.9 L)
1 c (340 g)	BOILED CIDER	5 c (1.7 kg)
1	CAMPDEN TABLET, IF NEEDED	5
½ pkg	ENGLISH ALE OR CIDER YEAST	1 pkg
½ tsp	PECTIC ENZYME POWDER	2½ tsp
Pkg instructions	YEAST NUTRIENT	Pkg instructions
½ oz (15 g)	OAK CUBES	2½ oz (70 g)
¼ c (60 ml)	BOURBON	1¼ c (300 ml)
½ to 1 tsp	POWDERED ACID BLEND, IF NEEDED	2½ to 5 tsp
⅛ to ½ tsp	POWDERED WINE TANNIN, IF NEEDED	¾ to 2½ tsp
2½ Tbsp (50 g)	MAPLE SYRUP, FOR BOTTLING	¾ c + 1 Tbsp (250 g)
¼ c (60ml)	HOT WATER, FOR BOTTLING	1 c (240 ml)

Combine a few cups of the juice and the boiled cider in a small saucepan. Warm over medium heat, stirring gently, until the cider has dissolved. Remove from the heat and let cool to room temperature.

Combine the boiled cider mixture and remaining juice in a sanitized fermentation bucket. Check and record the original gravity. (If using unpasteurized juice, crush the Campden tablet[s] and whisk into the juice; snap on the lid, insert an air lock filled with sanitizer or vodka, and let the juice stand for 24 hours.)

Sprinkle the yeast, pectic enzyme, and yeast nutrient over the juice. Whisk vigorously with a sanitized whisk to dissolve the ingredients and aerate the juice. Snap on the lid and insert a filled air lock. Place the bucket out of direct sunlight and at room temperature (70° to 75°F). Fermentation should begin within 24 hours (bubbles will pop regularly through the air lock). Active fermentation will peak after a few days, and then gradually finish within 1 to 2 weeks.

Meanwhile, combine the oak cubes and bourbon in a small container. Soak for at least 1 week, or until the cider has finished actively fermenting.

Once you've seen very little activity in the air lock for a few days (a stray bubble or two is fine), strain the oak cubes from the bourbon, reserving the bourbon. Transfer the oak cubes to a mesh bag and place in a sanitized jug or carboy. Siphon the cider over the top, leaving behind as much sediment as possible. As you transfer the cider, taste it using a sanitized wine thief to check its progress. Insert the stopper and air lock, then place the cider out of direct sunlight and at room temperature for another 2 weeks or up to 2 months. Taste regularly and remove the oak cubes when you like the flavor (you can also add the reserved bourbon for stronger flavor, if you'd like).

When ready to bottle, taste the cider again. If needed, add acid blend for more acidity or tannin for more astringency. Taste again a few days later, and continue adjusting and tasting until you're happy.

Check the final gravity and calculate the ABV. Dissolve the maple syrup in the hot water and mix with the cider, back-sweetening if desired (see page 52). Bottle the cider. Wait 2 weeks before drinking or store for up to a year. Serve chilled.

APPLE PILSNER

average abv: 8%

The hallmarks of a good pilsner lager are a clean and crisp flavor profile, a touch of malty sweetness, and very light hops. I add a little dark honey (like buckwheat honey) to give this pilsner-style cider a "malty" quality and then dry hop using Saaz hops, which are traditional for pilsners. The lager yeast for making pilsners works best at low temperatures, so use a temperature-controlled fridge if you have one, or wait until the temperature outside turns chilly and ferment the cider in your basement or garage.

1 GALLON	INGREDIENTS	5 GALLONS
1 gal (3.8 L)	APPLE JUICE	5 gal (18.9 L)
¼ c (85 g)	HONEY, ANY DARK, AMBER-HUED VARIETY	1¼ c (425 g)
1	CAMPDEN TABLET, IF NEEDED	5
½ pkg	PILSNER LAGER YEAST	1 pkg
½ tsp	PECTIC ENZYME POWDER	2½ tsp
Pkg instructions	YEAST NUTRIENT	Pkg instructions
⅕ oz (5 g)	SAAZ PELLET HOPS (3% AA)	1 oz (30 g)
½ to 1 tsp	POWDERED ACID BLEND, IF NEEDED	2½ to 5 tsp
⅛ to ½ tsp	POWDERED WINE TANNIN, IF NEEDED	¾ to 2½ tsp
2½ Tbsp (50 g)	HONEY, ANY VARIETY, FOR BOTTLING	Scant ¾ c (250 g)
¼ c (60ml)	HOT WATER, FOR BOTTLING	1 c (240 ml)

Combine a few cups of the juice and the honey in a small saucepan. Warm over medium heat, stirring gently, until the honey has dissolved. Remove from the heat and let cool to room temperature.

Combine the honey mixture and remaining juice in a sanitized fermentation bucket. Check and record the original gravity. (If using unpasteurized juice, crush the Campden tablet[s] and whisk into the juice; snap on the lid, insert an air lock filled with sanitizer or vodka, and let the juice stand for 24 hours.)

Sprinkle the yeast, pectic enzyme, and yeast nutrient over the juice. Whisk vigorously with a sanitized whisk to dissolve the ingredients and aerate the juice. Snap on the lid and insert a filled air lock. Place the bucket out of direct sunlight and at cellar temperature (55° to 60°F). Fermentation should begin within 24 hours (bubbles will pop regularly through the air lock). Active fermentation will peak after a few days, and then gradually finish within 1 to 2 weeks.

Once you've seen very little activity in the air lock for a few days (a stray bubble or two is fine), measure the hops into a mesh bag and place in a sanitized jug or carboy. Siphon the cider over the top, leaving behind as much sediment as possible. As you transfer the cider, taste it using a sanitized wine thief to check its progress. Insert the stopper and air lock, then place the cider out of direct sunlight and at cellar temperatures for another 2 weeks or up to 2 months. Taste regularly and remove the hops when you like the flavor.

When ready to bottle, taste the cider again. If needed, add acid blend for more acidity or tannin for more astringency. Taste again a few days later, and continue adjusting and tasting until you're happy.

Check the final gravity and calculate the ABV. Dissolve the honey in the hot water and mix with the cider, back-sweetening if desired (see page 52). Bottle the cider. Wait 2 weeks before drinking or store for up to a year. Serve chilled.

soft ciders

It's time to get to know the softer side of cider! By this I mean the low-alcohol and alcohol-free beverages that stand on the opposite end of the spectrum from the "hard" ciders in the previous chapters: sweet fresh-pressed cider, sparkling juices, and apple cider vinegars.

These projects are easy to make at home and don't require any extra equipment beyond what is already in your kitchen. Sparkling juices are usually ready in just a day or two, making them a fun diversion if you're waiting for a batch of cider to be ready. Cider vinegar and drinking vinegars (aka "shrubs") need a few weeks, but they're well worth the wait. Once you see how easy it is to make your own, it will be hard to go back to the store-bought stuff.

SWEET DRINKING CIDER

Fresh-pressed apple juice is a revelation. It's alive and vibrant and wonderful in a way that no mass-produced, store-bought apple juice can ever be. Every cider maker should try making some at least once, even if it's just a few cups that you make in a blender and squeeze through a cloth. The difference between this fresh apple juice and the stuff you usually find in a toddler's sippy cup is like night and day.

Aim for a mix of 2 parts sweet apples to 1 part tart apples in your juice. Even grocery store apples like Granny Smith and Gala make excellent juice. If you have some quinces, crabapples, or other bitter apples, by all means throw them in, but they're less essential for a quick juice blend like this. There's no minimum or maximum amount of juice you have to make. As a rough estimate, 20 pounds of apples will make about a gallon of juice.

Refrigerate your fresh apple juice immediately and drink within 1 to 2 days, or freeze it for several months. Even in the cool environment of the fridge, the juice will start to slowly ferment if left for longer. (You can drink it once it's started to ferment, of course! Just know that it will gradually become more alcoholic.)

JUICE IN A BLENDER OR FOOD PROCESSOR—
10 POUNDS (4.5 KG) OR LESS OF APPLES

Wash all the apples and thoroughly rinse them of any soap. Cut into quarters and trim away the cores and any large bruises or blemishes. Leave the peels on since they add some good flavor to the juice.

Pulse in a blender or food processer until no piece is larger than a pea. Transfer the pulp to a large mesh bag, and use your hands to squeeze out as much juice as you can into a clean bowl.

JUICE IN A JUICER—
20 POUNDS (9.1 KG) OR LESS OF APPLES

Wash all the apples and thoroughly rinse them of any soap. Cut into quarters and trim away the cores and any large bruises or blemishes. Slice the apples to a size that will fit through the tube of your juicer. Juice the apples according to your juicer's instructions and collect the juice.

JUICE USING A CIDER PRESS—
20 POUNDS (9.1 KG) OR MORE OF APPLES

Wash all the apples and thoroughly rinse them of any soap. Cut into quarters and trim away any large blemishes, but there's no need to remove the cores, seeds, or stems. Grind the apples into a pomace using a fruit masher, then press in your cider press according to the instructions that came with it.

SPARKLING APPLE JUICE

Sparkling apple juice is all about the fizz. Divide the juice among a few bottles, add a pinch of yeast, and put the cap on. In a day or two, you'll have a fizzy beverage that will rival any soda. You'll get a smidge of alcohol in your juice from this short ferment, but it's usually less than 1% ABV.

You can make your sparkling cider in reused soda bottles, swing-top homebrew bottles, or beer bottles of any size. (For reference, 1 gallon of juice will fill two 2-liter reused soda bottles.) Make sure they are clean and rinsed of soap, but since this project is so quick and you'll be drinking the juice right away, there is no need to sanitize—though you can if you want to!

You'll need some way to monitor the carbonation if you choose to use glass bottles. My trick is to include one small plastic soda bottle in the mix; when this bottle of juice feels rock-solid to the touch with the tiniest amount of give, it is carbonated. Since the juice in all the bottles carbonates at the same rate, this means that all your bottles should now be carbonated.

1 gal (3.8 L) apple juice   ¼ tsp dry champagne yeast

Clean all the bottles you will be using, including one small plastic soda bottle to use for monitoring the carbonation. Rinse the bottles thoroughly and line them up on a clean towel.

Pour a small amount of the apple the juice into a measuring cup and sprinkle the yeast over the top. Let stand, stirring once or twice, until the yeast has dissolved and then pour it back into the main container of juice. Shake gently to mix the yeast with the juice.

Use a small funnel to fill each bottle, leaving ½ to 1 inch of empty headroom at the top. Cap the bottles tightly and place them somewhere out of direct sunlight and at cool room temperature (around 70°F) to carbonate.

Check the small soda bottle twice a day to monitor the carbonation. When the plastic bottle feels rock solid with a tiny amount of give, carbonation is complete. Immediately refrigerate all the bottles to avoid overcarbonation and wait 24 hours before drinking. Carefully open the bottles over a kitchen sink or outdoors in case they fizz, and drink within a week.

SPARKLING CRAN-APPLE JUICE

Every Thanksgiving and every Christmas when we were kids, my brother and I would get to drink Martinelli's brand sparkling cider from tall, slender champagne flutes. It always felt so fancy, like we were almost grown-ups. I still love sparkling cider just as much today as I did then, but these days, I make my own.

This mix of cranberry juice and apple juice (pictured on page 118) is tart and refreshing, and it feels slightly more adult than straight sparkling apple juice. It also pairs well with a rich meal, so I like it as a nearly nonalcoholic alternative to wine or champagne at a dinner party. (You'll get a smidge of alcohol in your juice from this short ferment, but it's usually less than 1% ABV.)

Read more about what bottles to use and the carbonation process for making this recipe in the Sparkling Apple Juice headnote on page 122.

---

2 qt (1.9 L) apple juice

2 qt (1.9 L) cranberry juice

¼ tsp dry champagne yeast

Clean all the bottles you will be using, including one small plastic soda bottle to use for monitoring the carbonation. Rinse the bottles thoroughly and line them up on a clean towel.

Combine the apple juice and cranberry juice in a pitcher. Pour a small amount of juice into a measuring cup and sprinkle the yeast over the top. Let stand, stirring once or twice, until the yeast has dissolved and then pour it back in the pitcher. Stir gently to mix the yeast with the juice.

Use a small funnel to fill each bottle, leaving ½ to 1 inch of empty headroom at the top. Cap the bottles tightly and place them somewhere out of direct sunlight and at cool room temperature (around 70°F) to carbonate.

Check the small soda bottle twice a day to monitor the carbonation. When the plastic bottle feels rock solid with a tiny amount of give, carbonation is complete. Immediately refrigerate all the bottles to avoid overcarbonation and wait 24 hours before drinking. Carefully open the bottles over a kitchen sink or outdoors in case they fizz, and drink within a week.

SPARKLING GRAPE-APPLE JUICE

You can use either white grape juice or Concord grape juice for this recipe—you pick! White grape juice has a sweet and mild flavor, while Concord grape juice is more robust and has some nice puckery tannins. (You'll get a smidge of alcohol in your juice from this short ferment, but it's usually less than 1% ABV.)

Read more about what bottles to use and the carbonation process for making this recipe in the Sparkling Apple Juice headnote on page 122.

2 qt (1.9 L) apple juice

2 qt (1.9 L) white or red grape juice

¼ tsp dry champagne yeast

Clean all the bottles you will be using, including one small plastic soda bottle to use for monitoring the carbonation. Rinse the bottles thoroughly and line them up on a clean towel.

Combine the apple juice and grape juice in a pitcher. Pour a small amount of juice into a measuring cup and sprinkle the yeast over the top. Let stand, stirring once or twice, until the yeast has dissolved and then pour it back in the pitcher. Stir gently to mix the yeast with the juice.

Use a small funnel to fill each bottle, leaving ½ to 1 inch of empty headroom at the top. Cap the bottles tightly and place them somewhere out of direct sunlight and at cool room temperature (around 70°F) to carbonate.

Check the small soda bottle twice a day to monitor the carbonation. When the plastic bottle feels rock solid with a tiny amount of give, carbonation is complete. Immediately refrigerate all the bottles to avoid overcarbonation and wait 24 hours before drinking. Carefully open the bottles over a kitchen sink or outdoors in case they fizz, and drink within a week.

REAL CIDER VINEGAR

Vinegar is actually the natural ending point for a batch of cider—cider's grand finale, if you will. Cider becomes vinegar if it's left exposed to air after fermentation is complete. It eventually picks up a strain of bacteria called *Acetobacter*, which begins converting the alcohol in the cider into acetic acid and eventually transforms your hard cider into cider vinegar. This can happen accidentally if the seals on your bucket, jug, or carboy aren't quite tight or your air lock runs dry, or you can encourage it to happen intentionally by leaving the cider exposed to air. Making vinegar is a great way to salvage a mediocre batch of cider—much better than pouring it down the drain.

This process will happen on its own over time, but you can give it a kick-start by adding some premade raw (unpasteurized) vinegar. Use the ratio of hard cider to raw vinegar in this recipe and scale it up or down to change the amount of vinegar you want to make. Metal can give your vinegar a metallic flavor, so avoid using metal utensils.

1 qt (0.9 L) hard cider

¼ c (60 ml) raw cider vinegar, such as Bragg's

Combine the cider and vinegar in a clean glass container, such as a canning jar. Stir vigorously with a wooden or plastic spoon until the cider becomes frothy.

Cover the mouth of the jar with a clean, tightly woven dishtowel or cloth napkin secured with a rubber band. Place the jar somewhere out of direct sunlight, at room temperature (70° to 75°F), and away from any other fermentation projects.

Let the liquid stand until it turns into vinegar, 3 to 6 weeks. Check occasionally. You may see a white- or beige-colored film forming on the surface; this is called the "mother," and it's a natural part of the vinegar process. If you see any mold forming on the surface, scoop it away and continue. (If your vinegar develops a mother, you can save the mother in a closed container in small amount of cider vinegar and use it in your next batch in place of the raw cider vinegar.)

When the liquid smells and tastes like tart cider vinegar, it's ready. Transfer it to a small, airtight container, like an old vinegar jar or a swing-top bottle. Store in a cool, dark cupboard and use within a year.

APPLE SCRAP CIDER VINEGAR

I keep a small zip-top bag full of apple cores, peels, and other scraps in my freezer, and I add to it every time I cut an apple for a snack or make a batch of cider. When I have enough to pack into a canning jar, I turn those scraps into vinegar. Essentially, this works by mixing the scraps with water and sugar, letting it ferment, and then ignoring it until the liquid turns into vinegar. The resulting vinegar is slightly less intense and flavorful than the "real" vinegar in the recipe on page 127, but still perfectly tasty for making everything from salad dressing to tri-tip marinade.

Use this ratio of scraps, water, sugar, and raw vinegar and scale it up or down to change the amount of vinegar you want to make. You can skip the raw vinegar altogether if you have trouble finding some—it just helps speed things along. Metal can give your vinegar a metallic flavor, so avoid using metal utensils.

2 c (230 g) packed
apple scraps

1 qt (0.9 L) warm water

½ c (100 g) white sugar

¼ c (60 ml) raw cider
vinegar, such as Bragg's
(optional)

Pack the apple scraps into a clean glass container, such as a canning jar, leaving about 4 inches of headroom. Combine the water and sugar and stir until the sugar dissolves. Pour the sugar-water over the apple scraps. Cover the scraps by an inch or two, but leave a few inches of headroom in the jar.

Cover the mouth of the jar with a clean, tightly woven dishtowel or cloth napkin secured with a rubber band. Place the jar somewhere out of direct sunlight, at room temperature (70° to 75°F), and away from any other fermentation projects.

After a few days, you will see the liquid begin to bubble and ferment. Stir the liquid daily and push the apple scraps back under the surface. This prevents mold from forming, but if any does, you can just scoop it away before stirring the scraps.

When the bubbling slows, strain the liquid to remove the apple scraps, and transfer the liquid to a new jar. If you'd like to speed up the vinegar process, add the raw cider now. Stir the liquid vigorously with a wooden or plastic spoon until it becomes foamy. Re-cover the jar with the cloth and secure with a rubber band.

Let the liquid stand until it turns into vinegar, 3 to 6 weeks. Check occasionally. You may see a white- or beige-colored film forming on the surface; this is called the "mother" and it's a natural part of the vinegar process. If you see any mold forming on the surface, scoop it away and continue. (If your vinegar develops a mother, you can save it in a closed container in small amount of cider vinegar and use it in your next batch in place of the raw cider vinegar.)

When the liquid smells and tastes like tart cider vinegar, it's ready. Transfer it to a small, airtight container, like an old vinegar jar or a swing-top bottle. Store in a cool, dark cupboard and use within a year.

SPICED APPLE SHRUB

No, I'm not talking about those green bushy things bordering your lawn. I'm talking about an intensely sweet and intensely tart syrup made of vinegar, sugar, and fresh fruit. Mixed with sparkling water or shaken into a cocktail, that intensity will transform any drink—boozy or otherwise—into something you can't stop sipping. This particular shrub adds cinnamon and ginger for a warm, spicy twist. It's particularly good mixed with bourbon or rum for a winter cocktail. Metal can give your vinegar a metallic flavor, so avoid using metal utensils and place wax paper over the jar if using a metal lid.

To serve, mix 1 to 4 tablespoons with a glass of sparkling water or shake into a cocktail.
Taste and add more syrup, if you'd like.

2 to 3 large apples

1 (3-in) stick cinnamon

1 (2-in) piece fresh ginger, grated or finely diced

Peel stripped from 1 large orange

1 c (220 g) Demerara or brown sugar

1½ to 2 c (360 to 480 ml) cider vinegar, any kind

Cut the apples into quarters and trim away the cores. Shred or finely dice the apples. Transfer to a large glass container with a lid, such as a canning jar. Add the cinnamon stick, ginger, orange peel, and sugar. Pour the vinegar over the top until the ingredients are covered by an inch or two.

Cover the mouth of the jar with wax paper and screw on the lid. Shake vigorously to combine the ingredients and dissolve the sugar. It's fine if the sugar doesn't completely dissolve; it will gradually do so over the next few days.

Place the jar somewhere out of direct sunlight and at room temperature (70° to 75°F) for 2 to 7 days. Shake the jar daily and taste occasionally. Once the shrub has infused to your liking, strain and transfer to a clean jar. Store in the refrigerator and use within 6 months.

DRAGON'S BREATH FIRE CIDER VINEGAR

If you're feeling a bit sniffily or off your game after a night of kicking back too many ciders, a shot
of fire cider will set you right. This vinegar-based folk remedy is infused with all sorts of things guaranteed
to clear out your sinuses and pop your eyes open, from hot chile peppers to horseradish. You can shoot
it straight, or try stirring a few spoonfuls into warm water, tea, or sparkling water for a less jolting
experience. It also makes a great addition to marinades and salad dressings.

Use the ingredients and proportions here as a starting point, and then adjust based on your personal
taste or what you have in the kitchen. Fresh herbs like rosemary or sage, citrus like grapefruit or oranges,
and spices like cinnamon and cloves all make great additions to the base recipe. No need to peel the
root vegetables, but make sure they're scrubbed clean. Metal can give your vinegar a metallic flavor,
so avoid using metal utensils and place wax paper over the jar if using a metal lid.

½ c (70 g) finely diced
fresh ginger

½ c (70 g) finely diced
fresh horseradish

½ c (70 g) finely
diced yellow onion

¼ c (55 g) minced garlic

¼ c (35 g) thinly sliced
hot chiles, such as jalapeño
or habanero

1 Tbsp whole black
peppercorns

1 whole lemon

2 to 3 c (480 to 720 ml)
cider vinegar, any kind

¼ c (85 g) honey

Pack the ginger, horseradish, onion, garlic, chiles,
and peppercorns into a clean glass container, such as
a canning jar. Zest and juice the lemon, and add both
to the jar. Pour the vinegar over the top until the
ingredients are covered by an inch or two.

Cover the mouth of the jar with wax paper and
screw on the lid. Shake vigorously to combine
the ingredients.

Place the jar somewhere out of direct sunlight and
at room temperature (70° to 75°F) for 2 to 6 weeks.
Shake the jar every few days and taste occasionally.
Once the fire cider has infused to your liking, strain
and transfer to a clean jar. Sweeten to taste using
the honey now, or wait until serving. Store in the
refrigerator and use within a year.

apple wines

Apple wine can be as dry and crisp as a Pinot Grigio or as sweet and sultry as a Chardonnay, but either way, it's a glorious thing. Imagine the purest essence of apple, mixed with sunshine, and poured into a glass. That, my friends, is apple wine.

Making wine out of apples is really no harder than making cider. All you do is add some extra fermentable sugar, which increases the alcohol content and kicks the cider into wine territory. The sugar can be regular table sugar, honey, maple syrup, or any other fermentable sugar that sounds tasty to you. Add a cup or two per gallon and you'll end up with something quite crisp; add more and you'll get a sweet dessert wine.

One thing to know about apple wines is that they take time. Active fermentation time is about the same as for cider, but apple wines often continue to slowly bubble for weeks before all the sugar is gone. After that, it's good to let the wine mellow and age for another few months, if not longer. A too-young apple wine can taste thin and disappointing, but give it some time and it will mellow into the golden liquid sunshine you've been yearning for.

CRISP APPLE TABLE WINE

average abv: 13%

This makes an excellent table wine, like the kind you'd serve with an alfresco dinner during the summer. When adjusting the flavor of the wine before bottling, aim for something like a Sauvignon Blanc. It should taste crisp and acidic, but not overly so. Don't be shy about using acid blend or tannin if you need to, and conversely, feel free to jump-start malolactic fermentation (see page 45) if you think it's finishing with too much tartness.

1 GALLON	INGREDIENTS	5 GALLONS
1 gal (3.8 L)	APPLE JUICE	5 gal (18.9 L)
2 c (400 g)	SUGAR	10 c (1.9 kg)
1	CAMPDEN TABLET, IF NEEDED	5
½ pkg	WHITE WINE YEAST	1 pkg
½ tsp	PECTIC ENZYME POWDER	2½ tsp
Pkg instructions	YEAST NUTRIENT	Pkg instructions
½ to 1 tsp	POWDERED ACID BLEND, IF NEEDED	2½ to 5 tsp
⅛ to ½ tsp	POWDERED WINE TANNIN, IF NEEDED	¾ to 2½ tsp

Combine a few cups of the juice and the sugar in a small saucepan. Warm over medium heat, stirring gently, until the sugar has dissolved. Remove from the heat and let cool to room temperature.

Combine the sugar mixture and remaining juice in a sanitized fermentation bucket. Check and record the original gravity. (If using unpasteurized juice, crush the Campden tablet[s] and whisk into the juice; snap on the lid, insert an air lock filled with sanitizer or vodka, and let the juice stand for 24 hours.)

Sprinkle the yeast, pectic enzyme, and yeast nutrient over the juice. Whisk vigorously with a sanitized whisk to dissolve the ingredients and aerate the juice. Snap on the lid and insert a filled air lock. Place the bucket out of direct sunlight and at room temperature (70° to 75°F). Fermentation should begin within 24 hours (bubbles will pop regularly through the air lock). Active fermentation will peak after a few days, and then gradually slow or stop within 2 to 3 weeks.

Once you've seen little activity in the air lock for a few days (occasional bubbles are fine), siphon the wine to a sanitized jug or carboy, leaving behind as much sediment as possible. As you transfer the wine, taste it using a sanitized wine thief to check its progress; it will likely taste quite sweet and boozy. Insert the stopper and air lock, then place the wine out of direct sunlight and at room temperature for another 4 weeks or up to a year. If waiting longer than 4 weeks, transfer the wine to a new container when sediment collects on the bottom of this one.

When ready to bottle, taste the wine again. If needed, add acid blend for more acidity or tannin for more astringency. Taste again a few days later, and continue adjusting and tasting until you're happy.

Check the final gravity and calculate the ABV. Bottle the wine. Wait at least 6 months from the start of fermentation before drinking or store for several years. Serve chilled.

GOLDEN DELICIOUS APPLE CHARDONNAY

average abv: 14%

Golden Delicious apples aren't particularly known for making great cider, but they do a fine job when turned into wine. I think of this as unoaked Chardonnay and use mild wildflower honey to underscore the flavors. You're not likely to find Golden Delicious juice at the store, so you'll need to find a way to juice or press your own apples. On the plus side, the apples tend to be inexpensive, so you can make this recipe without emptying your wallet.

1 GALLON	INGREDIENTS	5 GALLONS
20 lb (9 kg)	GOLDEN DELICIOUS APPLES	100 lb (45 kg)
2½ c (850 g)	HONEY, ANY LIGHT, AMBER-HUED VARIETY	12½ c (4.2 kg)
1	CAMPDEN TABLET	5
½ pkg	WHITE WINE YEAST	1 pkg
½ tsp	PECTIC ENZYME POWDER	2½ tsp
Pkg instructions	YEAST NUTRIENT	Pkg instructions
½ to 1 tsp	POWDERED ACID BLEND, IF NEEDED	2½ to 5 tsp
⅛ to ½ tsp	POWDERED WINE TANNIN, IF NEEDED	¾ to 2½ tsp

Wash all the apples and trim away any large bruises or damaged bits. Juice or press the apples as described in "Press Your Own Apples" (page 16).

Combine a few cups of the juice and the honey in a small saucepan. Warm over medium heat, stirring gently, until the honey has dissolved. Remove from the heat and let cool to room temperature.

Combine the honey mixture and remaining juice in a sanitized fermentation bucket. Check and record the original gravity. Crush the Campden tablet(s) and whisk into the juice; snap on the lid, insert an air lock filled with sanitizer or vodka, and let the juice stand for 24 hours.

Sprinkle the yeast, pectic enzyme, and yeast nutrient over the juice. Whisk vigorously with a sanitized whisk to dissolve the ingredients and aerate the juice. Snap on the lid and insert a filled air lock. Place the bucket out of direct sunlight and at room temperature (70° to 75°F). Fermentation should begin within 24 hours (bubbles will pop regularly through the air lock). Active fermentation will peak after a few days, and then gradually slow or stop within 2 to 3 weeks.

Once you've seen little activity in the air lock for a few days (occasional bubbles are fine), siphon the wine to a sanitized jug or carboy, leaving behind as much sediment as possible. As you transfer the wine, taste it using a sanitized wine thief to check its progress; it will likely taste quite sweet and boozy. Insert the stopper and air lock, then place the wine out of direct sunlight and at room temperature for another 4 weeks or up to a year. If waiting longer than 4 weeks, transfer the wine to a new container when sediment collects on the bottom of this one.

When ready to bottle, taste the wine again. If needed, add acid blend for more acidity or tannin for more astringency. Taste again a few days later, and continue adjusting and tasting until you're happy.

Check the final gravity and calculate the ABV. Bottle the wine. Wait at least 6 months from the start of fermentation before drinking or store for several years. Serve chilled.

SNOZZBERRY ROSÉ

average abv: 12%

The snozzberry scene from *Willy Wonka & the Chocolate Factory* made a huge impression on me as a kid. In this clip, the golden ticket winners discover wallpaper printed with lickable fruit, and Wonka encourages them to give it a try. "The snozzberries taste like snozzberries!" he says. Indeed. But what do snozzberries actually taste like? As a grown-up, I imagine they taste a lot like this blushing rosé wine: a mix of summer's best fruit.

1 GALLON	INGREDIENTS	5 GALLONS
3 qt (2.8 L)	APPLE JUICE	4 gal (15.1 L)
2 c (400 g)	WHITE SUGAR	10 c (2 kg)
1 c (340 g)	STRAWBERRIES, DICED	5 c (1.7 kg)
1 c (340 g)	PEACHES, DICED	5 c (1.7 kg)
1 c (340 g)	BLUEBERRIES	5 c (1.7 kg)
1 c (340 g)	BLACKBERRIES	5 c (1.7 kg)
1 c (340 g)	RASPBERRIES	5 c (1.7 kg)
1	CAMPDEN TABLET	5
½ pkg	RED OR WHITE WINE YEAST	1 pkg
½ tsp	PECTIC ENZYME POWDER	2½ tsp
Pkg instructions	YEAST NUTRIENT	Pkg instructions
½ to 1 tsp	POWDERED ACID BLEND, IF NEEDED	2½ to 5 tsp
⅛ to ½ tsp	POWDERED WINE TANNIN, IF NEEDED	¾ to 2½ tsp

Combine a few cups of the juice and the sugar in a small saucepan. Warm over medium heat, stirring gently, until the sugar has dissolved. Remove from the heat and let cool to room temperature.

Combine all the fruit in a large mesh bag and place in a sanitized fermentation bucket. With clean hands or a potato masher, mash the fruit to release their juices. Pour the cooled sugar mixture and remaining juice over the fruit. Check and record the original gravity. Crush the Campden tablet(s) and whisk into the juice; snap on the lid, insert an air lock filled with sanitizer or vodka, and let the juice stand for 24 hours.

Sprinkle the yeast, pectic enzyme, and yeast nutrient over the juice. Whisk vigorously with a sanitized whisk to dissolve the ingredients and aerate the juice. Snap on the lid and insert a filled air lock. Place the bucket out of direct sunlight and at room temperature (70° to 75°F). Fermentation should begin within 24 hours (bubbles will pop regularly through the air lock). Active fermentation will peak after a few days, and then gradually slow or stop within 2 to 3 weeks.

Once you've seen little activity in the air lock for a few days (occasional bubbles are fine), pull out the bag of fruit with clean hands and squeeze gently to extract as much liquid as possible. Insert a large funnel into the mouth of a sanitized jug or carboy and line it with cheesecloth. Slowly pour the wine into the jug, filtering out the solids. (Top off with additional apple juice if needed to fill the jug or carboy halfway up its curve.) Insert the stopper and air lock, then place the wine out of direct sunlight and at room temperature for another 4 weeks or up to a year. If waiting longer than 4 weeks, transfer the wine to a new container when sediment collects on the bottom of this one.

When ready to bottle, taste the wine again. If needed, add acid blend for more acidity or tannin for more astringency. Taste again a few days later, and continue adjusting and tasting until you're happy.

Check the final gravity and calculate the ABV. Bottle the wine. Wait at least 6 months from the start of fermentation before drinking or store for several years. Serve chilled.

APPLE PIE DESSERT WINE
average abv: 18%

You know that one family member who always sneaks back to the Thanksgiving pie table for "just one more slice"? That's me. I've never met a pie I didn't like, and this pie-flavored dessert wine is no exception. It's the combination of maple syrup, cinnamon, and vanilla bean that does it. Oh, and the bourbon. A small tumbler after dinner is as good as any dessert, or pour it over vanilla ice cream for a real treat.

Because you're adding so much maple syrup to this wine, you won't need as much apple juice to make a full 1-gallon or 5-gallon batch.

1 GALLON	INGREDIENTS	5 GALLONS
3 qt + 2 c (3.3 L)	APPLE JUICE	4 gal + 6 c (16.5 L)
3 c (935 g)	MAPLE SYRUP	15 c (4.6 kg)
1	CAMPDEN TABLET, IF NEEDED	5
½ pkg	WHITE WINE YEAST	1 pkg
½ tsp	PECTIC ENZYME POWDER	2½ tsp
Pkg instructions	YEAST NUTRIENT	Pkg instructions
1	VANILLA BEAN, WHOLE	4
2	3-INCH CINNAMON STICKS	6
2 Tbsp (30 ml)	BOURBON	½ c + 2 Tbsp (150 ml)
½ to 1 tsp	POWDERED ACID BLEND, IF NEEDED	2½ to 5 tsp
⅛ to ½ tsp	POWDERED WINE TANNIN, IF NEEDED	¾ to 2½ tsp

Combine a few cups of the juice and the maple syrup in a small saucepan. Warm over medium heat, stirring gently, until the syrup has dissolved. Remove from the heat and let cool to room temperature.

Combine the syrup mixture and remaining juice in a sanitized fermentation bucket. Check and record the original gravity. (If using unpasteurized juice, crush the Campden tablet[s] and whisk into the juice; snap on the lid, insert an air lock filled with sanitizer or vodka, and let the juice stand for 24 hours.)

Sprinkle the yeast, pectic enzyme, and yeast nutrient over the juice. Whisk vigorously with a sanitized whisk to dissolve the ingredients and aerate the juice. Snap on the lid and insert a filled air lock. Place the bucket out of direct sunlight and at room temperature (70° to 75°F). Fermentation should begin within 24 hours (bubbles will pop regularly through the air lock). Active fermentation will peak after a few days, and then gradually slow or stop within 2 to 3 weeks.

Once you've seen little activity in the air lock for a few days (occasional bubbles are fine), halve the vanilla bean and combine the bean pieces and cinnamon sticks in a mesh bag. Place the spice bag in a sanitized jug or carboy, add the bourbon, and siphon the wine over the top. As you transfer the wine, taste it using a sanitized wine thief to check its progress. Insert the stopper and air lock, then place the wine out of direct sunlight and at room temperature for another 4 weeks or up to a year. Taste regularly and remove the spice bag when you like the flavor. If waiting longer than 4 weeks to bottle, transfer the wine to a new container when sediment collects on the bottom of this one.

When ready to bottle, taste the wine again. If needed, add acid blend for more acidity or tannin for more astringency. Taste again a few days later, and continue adjusting and tasting until you're happy.

Check the final gravity and calculate the ABV. Bottle the wine. Wait at least 6 months from the start of fermentation before drinking or store for several years.

PEAR CHAMPAGNE

average abv: 10%

In the 1950s, a sweet and effervescent drink called Babycham started picking up popularity in Britain. This was, in fact, sparkling perry—not a recent invention by any means, but one that was now being rebranded as a glamorous, fun-loving drink for a new generation. In my homemade version, I like to use some wildflower or orange-blossom honey to give the perry an even more champagne-like flavor. Serve it in classic coupe glasses and put on some 1950s jazz music to get in the proper mood.

1 GALLON	INGREDIENTS	5 GALLONS
1 gal (3.8 L)	PEAR JUICE	5 gal (18.9 L)
1 c (430 g)	HONEY, ANY LIGHT AMBER-HUED VARIETY	5 c (1.7 kg)
1	CAMPDEN TABLET, IF NEEDED	5
½ pkg	CHAMPAGNE YEAST	1 pkg
½ tsp	PECTIC ENZYME POWDER	2½ tsp
Pkg instructions	YEAST NUTRIENT	Pkg instructions
½ to 1 tsp	POWDERED ACID BLEND, IF NEEDED	2½ to 5 tsp
⅛ to ½ tsp	POWDERED WINE TANNIN, IF NEEDED	¾ to 2½ tsp
Scant 3 Tbsp (60 g)	HONEY, ANY VARIETY, FOR BOTTLING	Scant 1 c (300 g)
¼ c (60ml)	HOT WATER, FOR BOTTLING	1 c (240 ml)

Combine a few cups of the juice and the honey in a small saucepan. Warm over medium heat, stirring gently, until the honey has dissolved. Remove from the heat and let cool to room temperature.

Combine the honey mixture and remaining juice in a sanitized fermentation bucket. Check and record the original gravity. (If using unpasteurized juice, crush the Campden tablet[s] and whisk into the juice; snap on the lid, insert an air lock filled with sanitizer or vodka, and let the juice stand for 24 hours.)

Sprinkle the yeast, pectic enzyme, and yeast nutrient over the juice. Whisk vigorously with a sanitized whisk to dissolve the ingredients and aerate the juice. Snap on the lid and insert a filled air lock. Place the bucket out of direct sunlight and at room temperature (70° to 75°F). Fermentation should begin within 24 hours (bubble will pop regularly through the air lock). Active fermentation will peak after a few days, and then gradually slow or stop within 2 to 3 weeks.

Once you've seen little activity in the air lock for a few days (occasional bubbles are fine), siphon the perry to a sanitized jug or carboy, leaving behind as much sediment as possible. As you transfer the perry, taste it using a sanitized wine thief to check its progress; it will likely taste quite sweet and boozy. Insert the stopper and air lock, then place the perry out of direct sunlight and at room temperature for another 1 to 2 months.

When ready to bottle, taste the perry again. If needed, add acid blend for more acidity or tannin for more astringency. Taste again a few days later, and continue adjusting and tasting until you're happy.

Check the final gravity and calculate the ABV. Dissolve the honey in the hot water and mix with the perry. Bottle the perry. Wait at least 6 months from the start of fermentation before drinking or store for several years. Serve chilled.

FIG AND HONEY DESSERT CYSER
average abv: 18%

Figs and honey are one of those culinary power couples that can do no wrong. Here, they make a show-stopping dessert cyser, best sipped slowly with plenty of pauses for good conversation and long-winded stories. I call it a *dessert* wine, but since it's so good paired with cheese, please feel free to pour it whenever and wherever a cheese plate is present.

Because you're adding so much maple syrup to this wine, you won't need as much apple juice to make a full 1-gallon or 5-gallon batch.

1 GALLON	INGREDIENTS	5 GALLONS
3 qt + 2 c (3.3 L)	APPLE JUICE	4 gal + 6 c (16.5 L)
2 c (680 g)	HONEY, ANY WILDFLOWER, CLOVER, OR ORANGE-BLOSSOM VARIETY	10 c (3.4 kg)
1	CAMPDEN TABLET, IF NEEDED	5
½ pkg	WHITE WINE YEAST	1 pkg
½ tsp	PECTIC ENZYME POWDER	2½ tsp
Pkg instructions	YEAST NUTRIENT	Pkg instructions
1 c (185 g)	DRIED MISSION FIGS	5 c (1.7 kg)
1	VANILLA BEAN, WHOLE	4
½ to 1 tsp	POWDERED ACID BLEND, IF NEEDED	2½ to 5 tsp
⅛ to ½ tsp	POWDERED WINE TANNIN, IF NEEDED	¾ to 2½ tsp

Combine a few cups of the juice and the honey in a small saucepan. Warm over medium heat, stirring gently, until the honey has dissolved. Remove from the heat and let cool to room temperature.

Combine the honey mixture and remaining juice in a sanitized fermentation bucket. Check and record the original gravity. (If using unpasteurized juice, crush the Campden tablet[s] and whisk into the juice; snap on the lid, insert an air lock filled with sanitizer or vodka, and let the juice stand for 24 hours.)

Sprinkle the yeast, pectic enzyme, and yeast nutrient over the juice. Whisk vigorously with a sanitized whisk to dissolve the ingredients and aerate the juice. Snap on the lid and insert a filled air lock. Place the bucket out of direct sunlight and at room temperature (70° to 75°F). Fermentation should begin within 24 hours (bubbles will pop regularly through the air lock). Active fermentation will peak after a few days, and then gradually slow or stop within 2 to 3 weeks.

Once you've seen little activity in the air lock for a few days (occasional bubbles are fine), coarsely chop the figs and halve the vanilla bean(s). Secure the figs and split bean(s) in a mesh bag, place in a sanitized jug or carboy, and siphon the cyser over the top. As you transfer the cyser, taste it using a sanitized wine thief to check its progress. Insert the stopper and air lock, then place the cyser out of direct sunlight and at room temperature for another 4 weeks or up to a year. Taste regularly and remove the figs and vanilla beans when you like the flavor. If waiting longer than 4 weeks, transfer the cyser to a new container when sediment collects on the bottom of this one.

When ready to bottle, taste the cyser again. If needed, add acid blend for more acidity or tannin for more astringency. Taste again a few days later, and continue adjusting and tasting until you're happy.

Check the final gravity and calculate the ABV. Bottle the cyser. Wait at least 6 months from the start of fermentation before drinking or store for several years.

ELDERFLOWER-PEAR DESSERT WINE

average abv: 15%

Last summer, a close friend acquired of a gargantuan bottle of St. Germain elderflower liqueur, and soon we were adding it to everything. This liqueur is made using tiny, fragrant elderflower blossoms, and its flavor reminds me of nibbling honeysuckle stems as a kid. A few ounces bumps up the floral sweetness of a perry (and the alcohol content), making this a dangerously good after-dinner sipper. This combination is also very nice with regular ciders. Just add a shot to your next glass of cider, perry, or sparkling cyser.

1 GALLON	INGREDIENTS	5 GALLONS
1 gal (3.8 L)	PEAR JUICE	5 gal (18.9 L)
2½ c (510 g)	HONEY, ANY LIGHT, AMBER-HUED VARIETY	15 c (5.1 kg)
1	CAMPDEN TABLET, IF NEEDED	5
½ pkg	WHITE WINE YEAST	1 pkg
½ tsp	PECTIC ENZYME POWDER	2½ tsp
Pkg instructions	YEAST NUTRIENT	Pkg instructions
1 c (240 ml)	ELDERFLOWER LIQUEUR, SUCH AS ST. GERMAIN	5 c (1.2 L)
½ to 1 tsp	POWDERED ACID BLEND, IF NEEDED	2½ to 5 tsp
⅛ to ½ tsp	POWDERED WINE TANNIN, IF NEEDED	¾ to 2½ tsp

Combine a few cups of the juice and the honey in a small saucepan. Warm over medium heat, stirring gently, until the honey has dissolved. Remove from the heat and let cool to room temperature.

Combine the honey mixture and remaining juice in a sanitized fermentation bucket. Check and record the original gravity. (If using unpasteurized juice, crush the Campden tablet[s] and whisk into the juice; snap on the lid, insert an air lock filled with sanitizer or vodka, and let the juice stand for 24 hours.)

Sprinkle the yeast, pectic enzyme, and yeast nutrient over the juice. Whisk vigorously with a sanitized whisk to dissolve the ingredients and aerate the juice. Snap on the lid and insert a filled air lock. Place the bucket out of direct sunlight and at room temperature (70° to 75°F). Fermentation should begin within 24 hours (bubbles will pop regularly through the air lock). Active fermentation will peak after a few days, and then gradually slow or stop within 2 to 3 weeks.

Once you've seen little activity in the air lock for a few days (occasional bubbles are fine), pour the elderflower liqueur into a sanitized jug or carboy and siphon the wine over the top. As you transfer the wine, taste it using a sanitized wine thief to check its progress. Insert the stopper and air lock, then place the wine out of direct sunlight and at room temperature for another 4 weeks or up to a year. (Sugars in the liqueur will renew fermentation for a few days, so you may see more bubbles in the air lock.) If waiting longer than 4 weeks, transfer the wine to a new container when sediment collects on the bottom of this one.

When ready to bottle, taste the wine again. If needed, add acid blend for more acidity or tannin for more astringency (or more elderflower liqueur for a stronger flavor). Taste again a few days later, and continue adjusting and tasting until you're happy.

Check the final gravity and calculate the ABV. Bottle the wine. Wait at least 6 months from the start of fermentation before drinking or store for several years. Serve chilled.

traditional ciders

England, Spain, and France are the historical epicenters of cider production, though other parts of the world (including North America) also have their own distinct cider cultures. These areas became known for their cider because this is where apples grew. After all, what do you do with an abundance of apples but make cider?

Each cider-making region has their own particular style, which evolved from the varieties of apples grown there, and slight variations in methodology. English ciders tend to be dry and tannic, Spanish ciders are usually sour and wild, and French ciders veer toward sweet and fizzy. The apples used to make these different ciders aren't typically found very far outside their native countries, so reproducing traditional ciders at home is largely an exercise in approximation.

I highly recommend seeking out commercial examples of these traditional ciders before you try making them. They have many qualities that are technically correct, but that can seem like flaws if you aren't expecting them, like the leathery, barnyard-like flavors from wild yeast fermentation or the strong earthy tannins from true bittersharp cider apples.

All of these ciders rely on wild yeast, predominantly *Saccharomyces*, in fresh-pressed apple juice for fermentation. If you're using store-bought juice or can't find the correct blend of apples for the recipe, I recommend adding *Brettanomyces* yeast (and sometimes *Lactobacillus* culture) in order to more closely approximate the flavors in traditional ciders. *Brett* isn't usually used in traditional cider making, but at home, it gets the job done.

Wild yeasts can linger on your equipment and infect other cider projects, so I suggest buying a second set for making the ciders in this chapter. Also, these ciders ferment best at cool temperatures; plan on making them during cooler months or use a temperature-controlled fridge.

TRADITIONAL FARMHOUSE CIDER
average abv: 6 to 8%

In the beginning, all cider was farmhouse cider. If you had an apple tree or two on your farm, you made cider—you didn't worry too much about the apple blend or the particular technique. You just pressed the apples and let the juice ferment with whatever wild yeast happened to be hanging around the farm.

To make your very own farmhouse cider, press some local apples or buy a few jugs of fresh, raw juice from a local orchard. Make sure it's not pasteurized—you want whatever wild yeast is hitching a ride with your apples. Cellar temperature is ideal during fermentation for best flavor; use a temperature-controlled fridge if you have one. Note that primary fermentation typically lasts 3 to 4 weeks at these cooler temperatures. Warmer temperatures mean a more rapid fermentation, which can give the cider a harsh flavor.

1 GALLON	INGREDIENTS	5 GALLONS
1 gal (3.8 L)	APPLE JUICE	5 gal (18.9 L)
½ tsp	PECTIC ENZYME POWDER	2½ tsp
Pkg instructions	YEAST NUTRIENT	Pkg instructions
½ to 1 tsp	POWDERED ACID BLEND, IF NEEDED	2½ to 5 tsp
⅛ to ½ tsp	POWDERED WINE TANNIN, IF NEEDED	¾ to 2½ tsp
3 Tbsp (25 g)	CORN SUGAR, FOR BOTTLING (OPTIONAL)	Scant 1 c (125 g)
¼ c (60ml)	HOT WATER, FOR BOTTLING (OPTIONAL)	1 c (240 ml)

Pour the juice into a sanitized fermentation bucket. Check and record the original gravity.

Sprinkle the pectic enzyme and yeast nutrient over the juice. Whisk vigorously with a sanitized whisk to dissolve the ingredients and aerate the juice. Snap on the lid and insert a filled air lock. Place the bucket somewhere cool (preferably 55° to 60°F). Fermentation should begin within a few days (bubbles will pop regularly through the air lock). If not, whisk in another dose of yeast nutrients and raise the temperature slightly until fermentation starts. Active fermentation will peak after a week or so, and then gradually finish within 3 to 4 weeks.

Once you've seen very little activity in the air lock for a few days (occasional bubbles are fine), siphon the cider to a sanitized jug or carboy, leaving behind as much sediment as possible. As you transfer the cider, taste it using a sanitized wine thief to check its progress. Insert the stopper and air lock, then place the cider somewhere cool for another 4 weeks or up to 6 months.

Taste occasionally and check the specific gravity to see how the cider is progressing. If your cider is very tart after active fermentation, wait for it to go through malolactic fermentation (or add malolactic culture; see page 45). The cider can be bottled whenever the specific gravity reaches +/-1.000.

When ready to bottle, taste the cider again. If needed, add acid blend for more acidity or tannin for more astringency. Taste again a few days later, and continue adjusting and tasting until you're happy.

Check the final gravity and calculate the ABV. Dissolve the corn sugar in the hot water and mix with the cider, if you'd like a sparkling cider (and a pinch of champagne yeast if you've aged your cider longer than 3 months). Bottle the cider. Wait 1 month before drinking or store for several years. Serve chilled.

CHEATER'S FARMHOUSE CIDER

average abv: 6 to 8%

If you can't get your hands on raw, fresh-pressed juice, you can still make a very respectable farmhouse-style cider using store-bought apple juice, commercial wild yeast culture, and *Lactobacillus* culture. Cellar temperature is ideal during fermentation for best flavor; use a temperature-controlled fridge if you have one. Warmer temperatures mean a more rapid fermentation, which can give the cider a harsh flavor.

1 GALLON	INGREDIENTS	5 GALLONS
1 gal (3.8 L)	APPLE JUICE	5 gal (18.9 L)
½ pkg	BRETTANOMYCES YEAST	1 pkg
½ pkg	LACTOBACILLUS CULTURE	1 pkg
½ tsp	PECTIC ENZYME POWDER	2½ tsp
Pkg instructions	YEAST NUTRIENT	Pkg instructions
½ to 1 tsp	POWDERED ACID BLEND, IF NEEDED	2½ to 5 tsp
⅛ to ½ tsp	POWDERED WINE TANNIN, IF NEEDED	¾ to 2½ tsp
3 Tbsp (25 g)	CORN SUGAR, FOR BOTTLING (OPTIONAL)	Scant 1 c (125 g)
¼ c (60ml)	HOT WATER, FOR BOTTLING (OPTIONAL)	1 c (240 ml)

Pour the juice into a sanitized fermentation bucket. Check and record the original gravity.

Sprinkle the yeast, *Lactobacillus*, pectic enzyme, and yeast nutrient over the juice. Whisk vigorously with a sanitized whisk to dissolve the ingredients and aerate the juice. Snap on the lid and insert a filled air lock. Place the bucket somewhere cool (preferably 55° to 60°F). Fermentation should begin within a few days (bubbles will pop regularly through the air lock). If not, whisk in another dose of yeast nutrients and raise the temperature slightly until fermentation starts. Active fermentation will peak after a week or so, and then gradually finish within 3 to 4 weeks.

Once you've seen very little activity in the air lock for a few days (occasional bubbles are fine), siphon the cider to a sanitized jug or carboy, leaving behind as much sediment as possible. As you transfer the cider, taste it using a sanitized wine thief to check its progress. Insert the stopper and air lock, then place the cider somewhere cool for another 4 weeks or up to 6 months.

Taste occasionally and check the specific gravity to see how the cider is progressing. If your cider is very tart after active fermentation, add malolactic culture to induce malolactic fermentation (see page 45). The cider can be bottled whenever the specific gravity reaches +/-1.000.

When ready to bottle, taste the cider again. If needed, add acid blend for more acidity or tannin for more astringency. Taste again a few days later, and continue adjusting and tasting until you're happy.

Check the final gravity and calculate the ABV. Dissolve the corn sugar in the hot water and mix with the cider, if you'd like a sparkling cider (and a pinch of champagne yeast if you've aged your cider longer than 3 months). Bottle the cider. Wait 1 month before drinking or store for several years. Serve chilled.

ENGLISH-STYLE CIDER

average abv: 6 to 8%

A good English cider is fairly dry and bracing in a way that encourages happy lip smacking. It shouldn't be aggressively tart or tannic, but there should be some amount of both. Above all, it should go well with pub food.

The method for making this cider is nearly identical to that for Traditional Farmhouse Cider (page 152). The difference really comes down to using English apple varieties. Look for Kingston Blacks, Cox's Orange Pippins, and Foxwhelps, or aim for a juice blend with a good amount of acidity and tannin. Unless you're able to find English apples, I recommend adding *Brettanomyces* yeast (even when using fresh-pressed juice) to encourage earthy, leathery, barnyard flavors in the finished ciders. Allow enough time for malolactic fermentation, and then bottle it still or with just a little priming sugar for a light effervescence.

1 GALLON	INGREDIENTS	5 GALLONS
1 gal (3.8 L)	APPLE JUICE	5 gal (18.9 L)
½ pkg	BRETTANOMYCES YEAST (OPTIONAL)	1 pkg
½ tsp	PECTIC ENZYME POWDER	2½ tsp
Pkg instructions	YEAST NUTRIENT	Pkg instructions
½ pkg	MALOLACTIC CULTURE	1 pkg
½ to 1 tsp	POWDERED ACID BLEND, IF NEEDED	2½ to 5 tsp
⅛ to ½ tsp	POWDERED WINE TANNIN, IF NEEDED	¾ to 2½ tsp
Scant 2 Tbsp (15 g)	CORN SUGAR, FOR BOTTLING (OPTIONAL)	Scant ⅔ c (75 g)
¼ c (60ml)	HOT WATER, FOR BOTTLING (OPTIONAL)	1 c (240 ml)

Pour the juice into a sanitized fermentation bucket. Check and record the original gravity.

Sprinkle the yeast, pectic enzyme, and yeast nutrient over the juice. Whisk vigorously with a sanitized whisk to dissolve the ingredients and aerate the juice. Snap on the lid and insert a filled air lock. Place the bucket somewhere cool (preferably 55° to 60°F). Fermentation should begin within a few days (bubbles will pop regularly through the air lock). If not, whisk in another dose of yeast nutrients and raise the temperature

slightly until fermentation starts. Active fermentation will peak after a week or so, and then gradually finish within 3 to 4 weeks.

Once you've seen very little activity in the air lock for a few days (occasional bubbles are fine), siphon the cider to a sanitized jug or carboy, leaving behind as much sediment as possible. As you transfer the cider, taste it using a sanitized wine thief to check its progress. Add the malolactic culture and gently swirl the jug or carboy to mix it in. Insert the stopper and air lock, then place the cider somewhere cool for another 4 weeks or up to 6 months.

Taste occasionally and check the specific gravity to see how the cider is progressing. The cider can be bottled whenever the specific gravity reaches +/-1.000.

When ready to bottle, taste the cider again. If needed, add acid blend for more acidity or tannin for more astringency—err on the side of more tannin for this cider. Taste again a few days later, and continue adjusting and tasting until you're happy.

Check the final gravity and calculate the ABV. Dissolve the corn sugar in the hot water and mix with the cider, if you'd like a sparkling cider (and a pinch of champagne yeast if you've aged your cider longer than 3 months). Bottle the cider. Wait 1 month before drinking or store for several years. Serve chilled.

SPANISH-STYLE SIDRA

average abv: 6 to 8%

Bring on the funk! Spanish sidras embrace all the sour and funky flavors that come from wild fermentation. This cider is also sometimes aged with oak or chestnut, which gives it a savory, woodsy flavor. It's even harder to find Spanish apples in North America than it is to find English or French, so aim for a good mix of mostly acidic and bitter apples. If your apple mix is lacking in these or if you're using juice, add both *Brettanomyces* yeast and *Lactobacillus* culture to get as much of that funky and sour flavor in your cider as you can. Let it go through malolactic fermentation, and then bottle it up.

1 GALLON	INGREDIENTS	5 GALLONS
1 gal (3.8 L)	APPLE JUICE	5 gal (18.9 L)
½ pkg	BRETTANOMYCES YEAST (OPTIONAL)	1 pkg
½ pkg	LACTOBACILLUS CULTURE (OPTIONAL)	1 pkg
½ tsp	PECTIC ENZYME POWDER	2½ tsp
Pkg instructions	YEAST NUTRIENT	Pkg instructions
½ pkg	MALOLACTIC CULTURE	1 pkg
½ oz (14 g)	OAK CUBES (OPTIONAL)	2½ oz (70 g)
¼ c (60 ml)	SPANISH WHITE WINE OR SHERRY (OPTIONAL)	1¼ cup (295 ml)
⅛ to ½ tsp	POWDERED WINE TANNIN, IF NEEDED	¾ to 2½ tsp

Pour the juice into a sanitized fermentation bucket. Check and record the original gravity.

Sprinkle the yeast, *Lactobacillus*, pectic enzyme, and yeast nutrient over the juice. Whisk vigorously with a sanitized whisk to dissolve the ingredients and aerate the juice. Snap on the lid and insert a filled air lock. Place the bucket somewhere cool (preferably 55° to 60°F). Fermentation should begin within a few days (bubbles will pop regularly through the air lock). If not, whisk in another dose of yeast nutrients and raise the temperature slightly until fermentation starts. Active fermentation will peak after a week or so, and then gradually finish within 3 to 4 weeks.

Once you've seen very little activity in the air lock for a few days (occasional bubbles are fine), siphon the cider to a sanitized jug or carboy, leaving behind as much sediment as possible. As you transfer the cider, taste it using a sanitized wine thief to check its progress. Add the malolactic culture and gently swirl the jug or carboy to mix it in. Insert the stopper and air lock, then place the cider somewhere cool for another 4 weeks or up to 6 months.

If you'd like an oaky flavor in your cider, soak the oak cubes for one week in the wine, then strain them and add to the cider at any point during this period. Taste the cider regularly, and remove the oak cubes or siphon the cider to a new container when infused to your liking. The cider can be bottled whenever the specific gravity reaches +/-1.000.

When ready to bottle, taste the cider again. If needed, add tannin for more astringency—this cider should taste slightly tart and with obvious tannins. Taste again a few days later, and continue adjusting and tasting until you're happy.

Check the final gravity and calculate the ABV. Bottle the cider. Wait 1 month before drinking or store for several years. Serve at room temperature or chilled.

COLONIAL NEW ENGLAND–STYLE CIDER

average abv: 8 to 10%

The apple trees of New England in the days of the first settlers were tough, rugged things that produced tart and bitter fruit without a lot of natural sugar. Cider makers sometimes added things like molasses, maple syrup, brown sugar, or raisins to help boost the sugar content and give the cider some flavor. Molasses in particular adds a slightly smoky flavor, like burnt sugar, to the cider. I love this flavor, but use another sugar if you're not a fan.

Happily, it's becoming easier to find some of the older North American apple varieties once prized for cider making. Keep your eyes open at farmers' markets for Baldwins, Cortlands, Gravensteins, Newtown Pippins, Roxbury Russets, and Winesaps. If you have fresh, unpasteurized juice, you can let this cider go through a natural yeast fermentation, like the Traditional Farmhouse Cider on page 152, or add *Brettanomyces* and lactobacillus culture for a more distinct funk. Let it go through malolactic fermentation and bottle still or carbonated.

1 GALLON	INGREDIENTS	5 GALLONS
1 gal (3.8 L)	APPLE JUICE	5 gal (18.9 L)
¼ c (85 g)	MOLASSES	1¼ c (425 g)
¾ c (130 g)	RAISINS, COARSELY CHOPPED	3 ¾ c (640 g)
½ pkg	BRETTANOMYCES YEAST (OPTIONAL) IF USING FRESH JUICE	1 pkg
½ pkg	LACTOBACILLUS CULTURE (OPTIONAL) IF USING FRESH JUICE	1 pkg
½ tsp	PECTIC ENZYME POWDER	2½ tsp
Pkg instructions	YEAST NUTRIENT	Pkg instructions
½ pkg	MALOLACTIC CULTURE	1 pkg
½ to 1 tsp	POWDERED ACID BLEND, IF NEEDED	2½ to 5 tsp
⅛ to ½ tsp	POWDERED WINE TANNIN, IF NEEDED	¾ to 2½ tsp
3 Tbsp (25 g)	CORN SUGAR, FOR BOTTLING (OPTIONAL)	Scant 1 c (125 g)
¼ c (60ml)	HOT WATER, FOR BOTTLING (OPTIONAL)	1 c (240 ml)

Combine a few cups of the juice, the molasses, and the chopped raisins in a small saucepan. Warm over medium heat, stirring gently, until the molasses has dissolved. Remove from the heat and let cool to room temperature.

Combine the molasses mixture and remaining juice in a sanitized fermentation bucket. Sprinkle the yeast, *Lactobacillus*, pectic enzyme, and yeast nutrient over the juice. Whisk vigorously with a sanitized whisk to dissolve the ingredients and aerate the juice. Snap on the lid and insert a filled air lock. Place the bucket somewhere cool (preferably 55° to 60°F). Fermentation should begin within a few days (bubbles will pop regularly through the air lock). If not, whisk in another dose of yeast nutrient and raise the temperature slightly until fermentation starts. Active fermentation will peak after a week or so, and then gradually finish within 3 to 4 weeks.

Once you've seen very little activity in the air lock for a few days (occasional bubbles are fine), siphon the cider to a sanitized jug or carboy, leaving behind as much sediment as possible. As you transfer the cider, taste it using a sanitized wine thief to check its progress. Add the malolactic culture and gently swirl the jug or carboy to mix it in. Insert the stopper and air lock, then place the cider somewhere cool for another 4 weeks or up to 6 months.

Taste occasionally and check the specific gravity to see how the cider is progressing. The cider can be bottled whenever the specific gravity reaches +/-1.000.

When ready to bottle, taste the cider again. If needed, add acid blend for more acidity or tannin for more astringency. Taste again a few days later, and continue adjusting and tasting until you're happy.

Check the final gravity and calculate the ABV. Dissolve the corn sugar in the hot water and mix with the cider, if you'd like a sparkling cider (and a pinch of champagne yeast if you've aged your cider longer than 3 months). Bottle the cider. Wait 1 month before drinking or store for several years. Serve chilled.

FRENCH-STYLE CIDRE DOUX (SWEET CIDER)

average abv: 5 to 6%

The French have mastered the art of the fizzy, naturally sweet, low-alcohol cider. They use a process called "keeving," which involves stripping away most of the nutrients and wild yeast from the apple juice before fermentation begins. This puts such a strain on the remaining yeast that it stops working before the cider is fully fermented, leaving you with a fairly sweet cider with relatively low levels of alcohol.

A true keeve is a fairly tricky endeavor on a home level. Here I give a modified method that slows down fermentation with cool temperatures and gradually culls the yeast population through weekly siphoning. If all goes well, fermentation will come to a standstill at a specific gravity of 1.015 or 1.010, and you'll have made a semidry cider.

Cider made this way is not as stable as one made with a true keeve, and it will likely begin fermenting again if the temperature is raised or sugar is added. While French ciders are naturally sparkling, plan on making a still cider, keep the cider chilled after bottling, and drink within a few months. To come even closer to a true *cidre doux*, seek out French cider apple varieties, like Muscat de Bernay or Reine des Reinettes.

1 GALLON	INGREDIENTS	5 GALLON
1 gal (3.8 L)	APPLE JUICE	5 gal (18.9 L)
½ pkg	BRETTANOMYCES YEAST, IF USING PASTEURIZED JUICE	1 pkg
½ pkg	LACTOBACILLUS CULTURE, IF USING PASTEURIZED JUICE	1 pkg
½ tsp	PECTIC ENZYME POWDER	2½ tsp
½ to 1 tsp	POWDERED ACID BLEND, IF NEEDED	2½ to 5 tsp
⅛ to ½ tsp	POWDERED WINE TANNIN, IF NEEDED	¾ to 2½ tsp

Pour the juice into a sanitized fermentation bucket. Check and record the original gravity.

Sprinkle the yeast, *Lactobacillus*, and pectic enzyme over the juice. Whisk vigorously with a sanitized whisk to dissolve the ingredients and aerate the juice. Snap on the lid and insert a filled air lock. Place the bucket somewhere cool (preferably 50° to 55°F).

Fermentation should begin within a few days (bubbles will pop regularly through the air lock). If not, raise the temperature slightly until fermentation starts, then lower again once active.

After 1 week, regardless of how much fermentation activity you see, siphon the cider to a sanitized jug or carboy, leaving behind as much sediment as possible. As you transfer the cider, taste it using a sanitized wine thief and check the specific gravity to monitor its progress. Insert the stopper and air lock, then place the cider somewhere cool.

Continue siphoning the cider to a new jug or carboy every week until the specific gravity remains the same for several weeks in a row. Add acid blend for more acidity or tannin for more astringency at any point.

Once the specific gravity is stable, bottle the cider. Keep the bottles chilled to avoid refermentation, and drink within 6 months.

CHEATER'S CIDRE DOUX (SWEET CIDER)
average abv: varies

If the French-Style Cidre Doux (page 163) sounds like too much hassle, there is another option for making a sweet cider: let the cider ferment as normal, neutralize the remaining yeast with stabilizers or through pasteurization, and then add as much additional apple juice as you like. Since the yeast is gone, the juice will sweeten and dilute the alcohol content without causing renewed fermentation.

The methods outlined in this recipe can also be used to sweeten any recipe in this book and are described in more detail in "Step Six: Make Final Adjustments and Back-Sweeten Your Cider" on page 51. This cider must be bottled and served as a still beverage to avoid risk of renewed fermentation and overcarbonated bottles.

1 GALLON	INGREDIENTS	5 GALLONS
1 gal (3.8 L)	APPLE JUICE	5 gal (18.9 L)
½ pkg	BRETTANOMYCES YEAST, IF USING PASTEURIZED JUICE	1 pkg
½ pkg	LACTOBACILLUS CULTURE, IF USING PASTEURIZED JUICE	1 pkg
½ tsp	PECTIC ENZYME POWDER	2½ tsp
Pkg instructions	YEAST NUTRIENT	Pkg instructions
1	CAMPDEN TABLET, CRUSHED	5
½ tsp	POTASSIUM SORBATE	2½ tsp
½ to 1 tsp	POWDERED ACID BLEND, IF NEEDED	2½ to 5 tsp
⅛ to ½ tsp	POWDERED WINE TANNIN, IF NEEDED	¾ to 2½ tsp
	ADDITIONAL PASTEURIZED APPLE JUICE, TO BACK-SWEETEN	

Pour the juice into a sanitized fermentation bucket. Check and record the original gravity.

Sprinkle the yeast, *Lactobacillus*, pectic enzyme, and yeast nutrient over the juice. Whisk vigorously with a sanitized whisk to dissolve the ingredients and aerate the juice. Snap on the lid and insert a filled air lock.

Place the bucket somewhere cool (preferably 55° to 60°F). Fermentation should begin within a few days (bubbles will pop regularly through the air lock). If not, whisk in another dose of yeast nutrient and raise the temperature slightly until fermentation starts. Active fermentation will peak after a week or so, and then gradually finish within 3 to 4 weeks.

Once you've seen very little activity in the air lock for a few days (occasional bubbles are fine), siphon the cider to a sanitized jug or carboy, leaving behind as much sediment as possible. As you transfer the cider, taste it using a sanitized wine thief to check its progress. Insert the stopper and air lock, then place the cider somewhere cool for another 4 weeks or up to 6 months.

Taste occasionally and check the specific gravity to see how the cider is progressing. The cider can be back-sweetened whenever the specific gravity reaches +/-1.000.

To treat the cider with stabilizers: Siphon the cider to a new jug or carboy, leaving behind as much sediment as possible. Crush the Campden tablet(s), sprinkle over the top, and swirl gently to dissolve. Wait 24 hours for the Campden to work, then add the potassium sorbate. Swirl gently to dissolve, and wait another 24 hours.

Sweeten the cider to taste using additional apple juice. Wait a week or two before bottling and watch for any signs of refermentation. (If fermentation does begin again, let it carry out before making another attempt at back-sweetening or bottling.)

Check the final gravity and calculate the ABV. Bottle the cider. Wait 2 weeks before drinking or store for up to a year. If any bottles burst or you see any signs of carbonation when you open a bottle, refrigerate all bottles immediately and drink them within a few weeks.

To pasteurize the cider: On the day you plan to pasteurize and bottle the cider, sweeten it to taste with additional apple juice. Check the final gravity and calculate the ABV. Immediately transfer the cider to bottles, but do not cap.

Place all the bottles in a stockpot (working in batches if necessary). Fill the stockpot with water up to the necks of the bottles and set the stockpot over medium heat. Warm until the cider inside the center bottle registers 160°F. Turn the heat to low and hold the temperature of the cider between 160° and 165°F for 5 minutes to pasteurize.

Remove the bottles from the water and cool completely before capping. Wait 2 weeks before drinking or store for up to a year. If any bottles burst or you see any signs of carbonation when you open a bottle, refrigerate all bottles immediately and drink them within a few weeks.

TROUBLESHOOTING YOUR HOMEMADE CIDER

Fermentation plays by its own rules and sometimes things pop up that can't be anticipated. Here are the most typical situations that can happen while making a batch of cider, and what to do about them.

IF YOU FORGOT TO SANITIZE YOUR EQUIPMENT

The number-one cause of a spoiled batch of cider is an infection introduced through poor sanitation practices. Get in the habit of sanitizing everything. Obsessively. Always. It's better to be overly cautious about sanitation than to scrimp and wind up with an infection.

This said, if your sanitation is generally good and you accidentally slip up one time, then your cider is probably fine. Yes, there's a little risk that some nasty bacteria slipped in, but probably not. Until you actually see any signs of infection, continue making the cider as usual.

IF YOU ADDED SULFITES, BUT CAN'T WAIT 24 HOURS FOR THEM TO DISSIPATE

Sulfites take a full 24 hours to clear the cider of any wild yeast or bacteria and then dissipate. If you add the commercial yeast much before the 24 hours are up, any sulfites lingering around might interfere with the start of fermentation. If at all possible, wait a full 24 hours before adding the yeast or up to 36 hours. If you have to add the yeast early for any reason, go ahead and do so, but keep an eye on it. If fermentation doesn't start within a day or two, add more yeast.

IF YOU ADDED SULFITES, BUT FORGOT TO ADD THE YEAST

If it's been less than 36 hours, the juice is fine—go ahead and add the yeast. If it's been more than 36 hours, check your juice for any signs of mold or aromas of spoilage. If it seems okay, you can continue. If you're unsure, it might be a good idea to add another dose of sulfites to clear out anything that might have started growing (and then remember to add the yeast).

The 36-hour maximum is a little arbitrary here. Sulfites preserve the juice up to a point, but not indefinitely. You're usually safe within 36 hours, but beyond that, it can get chancy. Use your best judgment.

IF YOU FORGOT TO PUT LIQUID IN YOUR AIR LOCK

Add sanitizer, vodka, or water up to the "fill line" as soon as you remember. There's a small chance that your cider picked up an infection while it was unprotected, but if you caught it within a day or two and fermentation seems to be going strong, you're probably fine. Keep an eye out for signs of infections over the next few weeks (such as weird smells, weird tastes, weird fuzz growing on the surface of the liquid).

IF YOU DON'T SEE ANY BUBBLES IN YOUR AIR LOCK AFTER 24 HOURS

Did you remember to add the yeast? You'd be surprised how often this has happened to me, so don't feel sheepish. Just go ahead and add the yeast as soon as you remember. Also, if you're fermenting the cider with wild yeast, remember that fermentation can take a little longer to start. Wait a few more days before you panic.

Is it chilly in your house? If it's below 65°F, then the yeast can be a little sluggish and slow to get started. Move the cider somewhere warmer, if possible.

If fermentation still hasn't started, then the culprit might be a bad batch of yeast. Pick up some new yeast as soon as you can, double-check the expiration date, and add it to your cider.

IF THE BUBBLING SLOWS DOWN OR STOPS SOONER THAN YOU EXPECTED

This usually means that the active stage of fermentation is close to, or has already, finished. Congrats, you've made cider! If it's warm in your house, this stage could happen in just a few days. Let the cider sit for a little longer to give the sediment time to settle, and then transfer it to the jug or carboy.

IF YOU WERE GONE FOR A FEW DAYS AND AREN'T SURE IF FERMENTATION HAPPENED

In all likelihood, fermentation did indeed happen and has now slowed or stopped. Check the specific gravity of your cider and give it a taste. If fermentation occurred, then the specific gravity will be significantly lower than when you started. The cider will also taste much less sweet and closer to hard cider.

IF THE BUBBLING DOESN'T STOP

Most ciders will finish fermenting within a few weeks and you'll see no more bubbles in the air lock. But some ciders take a little longer, especially ones made with wild yeast or that have extra sugar added. If the cider still looks, smells, and tastes okay, then let it continue. Keep a close eye on it and take samples every week or so to check that everything is okay. Malolactic fermentation can also cause some renewed bubble action in the air lock.

In some cases, nonstop bubbling can mean the cider has picked up an infection. This cider will start to smell and taste very disgusting and spoiled, and you might notice mold or oily residue on the surface of the cider. If this happens, it's best to toss the batch and start again.

IF THE TEMPERATURE IN YOUR HOUSE IS VERY HOT OR VERY COLD

Yeast is a pretty tolerant organism and will generally do fine at temperatures ranging from 65° to 85°F. Above 85°F, the yeast will still work, but it gets stressed out and you'll start to notice some unpleasant flavors in your cider. If possible, move the cider somewhere cooler, or wrap it in water-soaked towels. On extremely hot days, you can also tuck ice packs into the wet towels to keep the cider cool.

If the temperature drops below 65°F, then move your cider to the warmest spot you can find. You can place it near a heater or furnace, or place the cider on a heating pad, but be careful the cider doesn't get too hot. Homebrewing stores also sell special heating pads and wraps for buckets and carboys.

IF YOU FORGOT YOUR CIDER IN THE PRIMARY FERMENTATION BUCKET AND HAVEN'T TRANSFERRED IT TO THE GLASS JUG OR CARBOY

That's fine! If it's been over a month, fermentation seems complete, and the cider tastes good to you, then go ahead and bottle it. Otherwise, transfer it to a jug or carboy and let it age a little longer. If it's been a few months or more in the primary, you might start to notice some odd vegetal flavors caused by the decomposing sediment at the bottom of the bucket or oxidized sherry-like flavors from air seeping through the plastic. If the taste is faint, you can carry on. If it's strong, then unfortunately there's not much to be done other than tossing the batch.

IF SOME SEDIMENT GETS TRANSFERRED TO THE JUG OR CARBOY WHILE SIPHONING

This is fine! The primary goal of transferring the cider from the bucket to the jug or carboy is to get it off *most* of the sediment. But if a little gets transferred as you're siphoning, it's no big deal. This sediment will quickly fall to the bottom of the jug or carboy in the next few days.

IF THERE'S A LOT OF SEDIMENT FLOATING IN YOUR CIDER THAT DOESN'T SEEM TO SETTLE

Try chilling the cider in a fridge or a very cold (but not freezing) part of your house. This is called "cold crashing," and it can sometimes force those stubborn floating particles to settle on the bottom. Cold crashing won't help if your problem is haziness in the cider, not solid particles, but it also won't hurt.

IF IT'S BEEN LONGER THAN 3 MONTHS BEFORE BOTTLING

This is totally fine, and your cider probably tastes even better for the wait. If you want to make a sparkling cider, then be sure to add some new yeast when you bottle because any yeast from earlier in the process has died by now. Use the same yeast in the same amount as at the beginning of fermentation (or use champagne yeast if your cider was naturally fermented).

IF THERE IS MOLD ON THE SURFACE OF YOUR CIDER

This usually occurs only at the beginning of the cider-making process and happens when there is a problem with the yeast. Either you forgot to add the yeast, the yeast was expired, or, if it was a wild yeast fermentation, the yeast didn't get going quick enough before spoilage-causing bacteria took over. In all these cases, you'll need to throw away the juice and start over.

The only time you might get mold on a cider that's already gone through primary fermentation is if it has a very low alcohol content. Otherwise, the alcohol and the low pH of the cider keep it pretty well protected from molds and other spoilage bacteria.

IF YOU NOTICE A WHITISH FILM ON THE SURFACE OF YOUR CIDER

This is called "flower sickness," and it's typically due to a spoilage-causing film yeast that develops in the presence of oxygen. It most often affects ciders that have been left in the jug or carboy a little too long, especially when there's a fair amount of head space at the top of the jug or if the air lock has gone dry. If left unattended, this yeast will eventually spoil the batch, making it taste watery and lifeless.

Happily, if you catch it early enough, flower sickness can be forestalled just by adding sulfites to the cider. First, siphon the cider to a new container, trying to disturb the film yeast as little as possible. Leave an inch of cider behind—it's a small sacrifice for clean cider. In the new container, add sulfites at a rate of one crushed Campden tablet per gallon of cider. Wait 24 hours, then either bottle or let the cider continue to age. If aging, top off the cider with some extra apple juice to reduce the head space and prevent a new flower sickness from taking hold. You may need to add more yeast to kick-start fermentation on the new juice.

IF YOUR CIDER ISN'T SWEET ENOUGH

Homemade ciders often finish very dry, meaning "not at all sweet." If it's a little too dry for your taste and you'd like to add a touch of sweetness, then back-sweeten using one of the methods described in "Step 6: Make Final Adjustments and Back-Sweeten Your Cider," page 51.

IF YOUR CIDER TASTES TOO TART

Try adding some malolactic bacteria (which you can buy at a homebrew store) and letting your cider go through malolactic fermentation. This converts the harsh malic acid in the cider into softer lactic acid, and will likely take the edge off of the tart flavor in your cider.

You can also blend this cider with another, sweeter cider. This will give you a cider with a better overall balance of flavors.

IF YOUR CIDER IS DISAPPOINTING—NOT AWFUL, BUT JUST NOT VERY EXCITING

If you haven't already done so, try adding some acid blend and/or some tannin to round out the flavors. Use a little at first, taste after a few days, and add more if needed. Often, this is all it takes to make a bland cider taste great.

If you've already done that, the next step is to give your cider some time. I've had some batches that tasted "meh" at first, but then blossomed into amazing ciders once I gave them time to mellow. Put your jug or carboy, or your capped bottles of cider, in the back of a closet and forget about them for a few months. Then try the cider again.

If the cider still doesn't meet your standards for excellence, you have two options. First, you can blend it with another batch of cider, perhaps one with more acidity. You could even intentionally make a cider with stronger flavors with the intention of blending it with this one.

Second, you can turn your cider into cider vinegar. Even a boring batch of cider makes great vinegar! Read about how to do this in Real Cider Vinegar on page 127.

The only reason to ever pour a cider down the drain is if it actually has become infected with spoilage-causing bacteria or yeast. At this point, it will not be merely "meh"—it will look, smell, and taste disgusting. There's no saving a cider like this, so down the drain it goes.

IF YOUR CIDER SMELLS OR TASTES LIKE VINEGAR

Congratulations, you've made vinegar! That may not have been your intent, but that's probably what you've got. The likely cause is *Acetobactor*, which is a genus of bacteria that can infect cider when it's exposed to air, turning alcohol into acetic acid (that is, vinegar). The brief moments of exposure to air during transferring and bottling usually aren't enough to trigger the reaction. Most likely, you left the cider for too long before bottling and either the air lock ran out of liquid or there was too much headroom in the jug or carboy.

You can't stop the conversion to vinegar once it's started, unfortunately. If there's only a slight vinegar flavor and the cider is still palatable, then drink it as soon as you can. If it's well on its way to vinegar, just embrace it and surprise your family with bottles of homemade cider vinegar this holiday season.

IF YOUR CIDER SMELLS LIKE SULFUR OR ROTTEN EGGS

The most likely cause for this unpleasant aroma is the yeast you used, a lack of yeast nutrients at the start of fermentation, or (occasionally) warm fermentation temperatures. Some types of wine yeast seem to be particular offenders.

When this has happened to me, I've found that the aroma dissipates on its own after a few weeks, even if the cider is already in bottles. If it persists after this time, you may be stuck with it. Either hold your nose while you drink or turn your cider into vinegar (see Real Cider Vinegar, page 127).

In future batches, you may want to try a different type or brand of yeast. Pay close attention to the amount of yeast nutrients you add and try to ferment the cider at cooler temperatures.

IF YOUR CIDER SMELLS LIKE GERANIUMS

Cider sometimes picks up a geranium aroma if it went through malolactic fermentation and then you later added potassium sorbate. The sorbic acid in the potassium sorbate reacts with the lactic acid left from the malolactic fermentation to create this odd aroma. Once this reaction happens, there's no going back.

You can drink your cider if the aroma isn't too distasteful to you, or you can turn your cider into vinegar (see Real Cider Vinegar, page 127). In future batches, avoid adding potassium sorbate if the cider went through MLF.

IF YOUR CIDER TASTES OR SMELLS LIKE OLD COOKING SHERRY OR DAMP CARDBOARD

A little sherry-like flavor isn't necessarily a bad thing, but if it starts to taste like something that's been in your grandma's cupboard for a few years, that means it has become oxidized. You're most likely to find this flavor or aroma in older, forgotten bottles of ciders and apple wines rather than fresh cider, but it can still sometimes happen if your cider is exposed to too much oxygen.

Drink all bottles as soon as you can once you discover this flavor or aroma. If the cider was still relatively young, this means your technique needs refining. In future batches, be careful of too much splashing during siphoning or leaving the cider exposed to air.

IF YOUR CIDER LOOKS HAZY

Did you make your cider with pasteurized juice? This juice will become lighter and more transparent over time, but sometimes won't become totally crystal clear. Your cider might also simply need more time. It will become clearer the longer it sits.

When pouring your cider, be careful not to disturb the thin layer of sediment at the bottom of the bottle and stop short of pouring it into your glass. This sediment isn't harmful to drink (in fact, it contains some good vitamins!), but it will make your cider hazy and give it a slightly yeasty flavor.

IF YOUR CIDER ISN'T FIZZY WHEN YOU OPEN THE BOTTLE

Did you remember to add the priming sugar when you bottled? The yeast needs this last bit of sugar in order to carbonate the cider in the bottle. Was your cider more than 3 months old when you bottled? Then it's likely there wasn't enough yeast left in the cider to carbonate it. If you think either of these is the case, you can either chalk it up to a learning experience and drink your cider as it is, or you can try uncapping all the bottles, adding a pinch of the missing ingredient, and then recapping.

Another possible reason for flat cider is storing your bottles somewhere a little too cool. Move them to a storage space that's around 70°F and let them sit for another two weeks to see if that helps them get fizzy.

IF YOUR CIDER WAS TOO FIZZY AND GUSHED OUT OF THE BOTTLE WHEN YOU OPENED IT

The most likely culprit here is that there was too much sugar in the cider when you bottled it, either because you added a little too much priming sugar or because the cider wasn't done fermenting. Refrigerate all bottles immediately to avoid the risk of exploding and be careful when opening them.

IF SOME OF YOUR BOTTLES EXPLODE

This is probably the same problem as above, just to a greater degree. Too much sugar means the yeast creates more carbonation, which creates too much pressure in the bottles and eventually causes them to explode. Refrigerate all unexploded bottles immediately and be very careful when opening.

Occasionally, gushing or exploding bottles are caused by an infection in the cider. If this is the case, you'll notice some pretty raunchy smells, tastes, or textures. This cider is best poured down the drain.

RESOURCES

supplies

CIDER SUPPLY (CIDERSUPPLY.COM): If you'd like to try your hand at the keeving process to make a true French-style cidre doux (see page 163), this site sells the necessary pectic methyl esterase (PME) and calcium chloride to home cider makers.

KING ARTHUR FLOUR (KINGARTHURFLOUR.COM): Check out this online baking supply store for ingredients like coconut flakes, vanilla beans, dried fruit, and boiled cider, if you're having trouble finding them elsewhere.

MOREBEER (MOREBEER.COM): This is a great online source for 1-gallon and 5-gallon fermentation equipment, as well as ingredients like yeast, powdered wine tannin, and acid blend. If you're in California, MoreBeer! has stores in Concord, Los Altos, Riverside, and San Leandro. See the website for details.

NORTHERN BREWER (NORTHERNBREWER.COM): This is another excellent online source for 1-gallon and 5-gallon fermentation equipment and cider-making ingredients.

PENZEYS SPICES (PENZEYS.COM): I've purchased all my spices for my homebrew projects from this online store for years. Their spices are dependably fresh, fragrant, and flavorful.

WESTON SUPPLY (WESTONSUPPLY.COM): I highly recommend Weston's fruit grinder and fruit press if you're thinking of investing in either piece of equipment. Both are very well made and easy for hobby cider makers to use.

books and publications

BREW YOUR OWN MAGAZINE (BYO.COM): Although primarily a magazine for beer brewers, it occasionally covers cider making and other topics that can be of interest to cider makers.

CIDERCRAFT MAGAZINE (CIDERCRAFTMAG.COM): This biannual publication primarily covers cider culture and cider industry news with the occasional piece on cider making, but there's plenty to inspire and educate an eager cider maker.

CIDER, HARD & SWEET: HISTORY, TRADITIONS, AND MAKING YOUR OWN BY BEN WATSON: Read this one for the history lesson. Watson goes all the way back to the BC era and shows how cider making evolved alongside empires and agriculture. This book also has incredibly comprehensive guides to North American, English, and European apple varieties.

CIDER MADE SIMPLE: ALL ABOUT YOUR FAVORITE DRINK BY JEFF ALWORTH: Here is an excellent introduction to the history, flavors, and fermentation methods of ciders from around the world. It's geared more toward drinking and appreciating cider than making it, but this is a great resource for new cider lovers or anyone attempting to make traditional ciders.

CIDER: MAKING, USING & ENJOYING SWEET & HARD CIDER BY LEW NICHOLS AND ANNIE PROULX: This book was originally published in 1980 and has become a classic for home cider makers in recent years. I found it a good resource for learning about cider apples and orchard practices.

CRAFT CIDER: HOW TO TURN APPLES INTO ALCOHOL BY JEFF SMITH: This is a straightforward and accessible introduction to making cider at home from the cider maker behind Bushwhacker Ciders in Portland, Oregon.

CRAFT CIDER MAKING BY ANDREW LEA: Lea provides a good overall introduction to cider making, but I keep it on my shelf for its chapter (a whole *chapter!*) on cider-making problems. From slimy pulp to mousey flavors, this book has an explanation for everything.

THE EVERYTHING HARD CIDER BOOK: ALL YOU NEED TO KNOW ABOUT MAKING HARD CIDER AT HOME BY DREW BEECHUM: I really appreciated Beechum's practical approach to present-day cider making when I first started experimenting with cider myself. His sense of humor and lack of pretention make the process feel accessible to anyone.

THE NEW CIDER MAKER'S HANDBOOK: A COMPREHENSIVE GUIDE FOR CRAFT PRODUCERS BY CLAUDE JOLICOEUR: This book is an essential resource for anyone wanting to refine their home cider-making skills or thinking of opening a commercial business. It goes into great detail on the technical aspects of cider making and has one of the most comprehensive descriptions of the French keeving process that I've come across.

community

AMERICAN HOMEBREWERS ASSOCIATION (HOMEBREWERSASSOCIATION.ORG): An organization and website dedicated to the promotion and education of American homebrewers, home mead makers, and home cider makers. They organize the National Homebrew Competition, which includes a section of homemade ciders.

CAMRA (CAMPAIGN FOR REAL ALE, CAMRA.ORG.UK): UK-based organization promoting traditional craft beer and cider.

HOME BREW TALK (HOMEBREWTALK.COM): Chat forum for homebrewers and cider makers of all levels to gather, ask questions, and share ideas.

UNITED STATES ASSOCIATION OF CIDER MAKERS (CIDERASSOCIATION.ORG): Organization for professional cider makers in the United States and organizers of the annual CiderCon.

events

CIDERCON (CIDERASSOCIATION.ORG): This annual conference is geared primarily toward professional cider makers, but should be on your radar if you're thinking of going pro.

CIDER GUIDE (CIDERGUIDE.COM): Hosted by Eric West, this site has a comprehensive guide to local cider festivals as well as an interactive map of cideries worldwide.

CIDER SUMMIT (CIDERSUMMITNW.COM): Sample your way through hundreds of craft ciders offered by producers from around the world at this festival. It's hosted in a few different cities each year; take a look at the website to find the nearest one to you.

GREAT LAKES INTERNATIONAL CIDER AND PERRY COMPETITION (GLINTCAP.ORG): This annual competition is open to both commercial and noncommercial (home) cider makers. The website is also a good resource for learning the particular style guidelines for different ciders.

PACIFIC NORTHWEST CIDER AWARDS (PNWCA.COM): The competition is open to commercial cider makers only, but is accompanied by a festival that is open to the public.

CIDER MAKER'S LINGO // A GLOSSARY

ACETIC ACID: The primary acid in vinegar, caused by *Acetobactor* conversion of alcohol to acetic acid. Its presence in cider is a major flaw and a sign that the cider is on its way to becoming vinegar.

ACIDIC APPLES: Apples with a high acid content.

ACIDITY: A primary flavor component in a good cider. The flavor should be tart or sour, not acetic.

ALCOHOL BY VOLUME (ABV): A measure of the alcohol content of cider.

BITTER APPLES: Apples with high levels of tannin.

CIDER APPLES: Historically, cider apples are bitter, tannic, astringent apples primarily used to make cider. Bittersharp apples also have a high acid content, and bittersweet apples also have a low acid content.

CYSER: A cider made with honey.

DRY HOPPING: Adding hops to a cider after primary fermentation is finished.

FERMENTABLE SUGARS: Sugars consumable by yeast to create alcohol and carbon dioxide. Examples are table sugar, honey, maple syrup, and agave nectar.

FINAL GRAVITY (FG): The specific gravity of the cider once all the fermentable sugars have been converted into alcohol and carbon dioxide.

KEEVING: A French method for producing a naturally sweet and low-alcohol cider by systematically depriving the yeast of nutrients.

LACTIC ACID: Malic acid is converted to lactic acid through malolactic fermentation. It has a softer, mellower flavor in the cider than malic acid.

MALIC ACID: The primary acid present in apples and apple juice. It has a sharp, tart flavor that is fine in balanced amounts, but can overwhelm a finished cider in larger quantities.

MALOLACTIC FERMENTATION (MLF): The process by which harsh malic acid is converted into milder lactic acid, giving you a cider with a more tempered acidity.

NATURAL FERMENTATION: Fermenting the cider using only the wild yeasts naturally present in raw, unpasteurized juice.

ORIGINAL GRAVITY (OG): The specific gravity of the cider before fermentation begins and before any sugars have been fermented into alcohol or carbon dioxide.

PASTEURIZATION: The process by which apple juice or cider is sterilized by heating the liquid to a specific temperature for a specific period of time.

PECTIN: A naturally occurring compound in apple flesh that can cause haziness in the finished cider unless removed. Pectin will not affect flavor.

PERRY: A cider made with pear juice

POMACE: Ground apple pulp before pressing.

PRIMING: Adding a small amount of fermentable sugar to a finished batch of cider in order to carbonate it in the bottle.

PRIMING SUGAR: Any fermentable sugar added to cider in order to cause carbonation in the bottle.

SPECIFIC GRAVITY: A measure of the density of liquid. In the case of cider, the gravity indicates the amount of dissolved sugar in the liquid.

SWEET APPLES: Apples with a high sugar content.

TANNIN: A naturally occurring compound that causes a sensation of bitterness, dryness, or astringency in the mouth. They are present in some apple skins and flesh, but can also be added as an extra ingredient.

UNFERMENTABLE SUGARS: Sugars that cannot be consumed by yeast or used to make alcohol or carbon dioxide. Examples include sucralose (Splenda), aspartame (Equal), and stevia.

WILD YEAST: The natural, native yeast living on apple skins and in raw, unpasteurized apple juice. The most common strain is *Saccharomyces*.

ACKNOWLEDGMENTS

As always after an endeavor like this, there are a great many people who need thanking. It takes a team to make a cookbook, after all. Without every single one of these people, the book in your hands would not have been possible.

To my husband, Scott: LUV U 4EVR +1

To my awesome family—Joyce and Dean (aka Mom and Dad), Andy and Darci, Jensen and Etta, Evelyn, Jessie and Bonnie, Russ and Ingrid, Jacqui and Alison: Giant bear hugs to each of you.

To my agent, Angela Miller: You're the cat's meow. I'm so glad to have you at my back.

To my team at Ten Speed—editor Lisa Westmoreland, designer Margaux Keres, and copyeditor Jean Blomquist: You are like a team of manuscript ninjas—stealthy, nimble, and perfect at your art.

To my photographer, Kelly Puleio: Thank you for making my ciders look so damn good. You are a true master at your craft.

To my stalwart crew of recipe testers—Jennifer Bannoura, Sheri Codiana, Dan Fick, Casey Fleishman, Owen Imholte, Will Imholte, David and Hilary Kahl, Amber Lucas, Ryan Payne, Mark Price, Gilbert Seward, Maggie Smith, Sam Smith, Charles Thresher, Ida Walker, and Philip Williamson: I raise my glass to all you fine and talented people, especially those of you who have now been with me through several projects.

To the cider makers who graciously shared their stories and answered so many cider questions: Scott Heath at Tilted Shed Ciderworks, Colin Davis at Shacksbury Cider, Mark McTavish at 101 Cider House, and Dave Takush at 2 Towns Ciderhouse.

To Duke Geren: Thank you, forever and always, for being my technical expert on all things ferment-y.

To Rainbow Orchards: A great many gallons of your fresh-pressed apple juice went into the making of this book. Whatever you are doing to your apples over there, don't ever stop.

To the Ladies of the South Bay Salon—Sheri Codiana, Coco Morante, Cheryl Sternman Rule, Michelle Tam, and Danielle Tsi: You are the best friends a gal could have, fartoots and all.

ABOUT THE AUTHOR

Emma Christensen is the managing editor for *Simply Recipes* and a dedicated homebrewer. She is the author of two additional books on homebrewing, *True Brews* and *Brew Better Beer*, and she collaborated on the James Beard Award–winning *The Kitchn Cookbook*. Her work has appeared in *Brew Your Own*, *Fine Cooking*, *Vegetarian Times*, *Cook's Country*, *Edible Columbus*, and *Edible Silicon Valley*. Emma is a graduate of The Cambridge School for Culinary Arts and Bryn Mawr College. She lives in San Jose, California. Find more great brewing projects at TheBoldBrewer.com.

INDEX

Published in the United States by Ten Speed Press,
an imprint of the Crown Publishing Group, a division
of Penguin Random House LLC, New York.

www.crownpublishing.com
www.tenspeed.com

Ten Speed Press and the Ten Speed Press
colophon are registered trademarks of Penguin
Random House LLC.

Library of Congress Cataloging-in-Publication
Data is on file with the publisher.

Hardcover ISBN: 978-1-60774-968-4
eBook ISBN: 978-1-60774-969-1

Printed in China

Design by Margaux Keres
Prop Stylist Natasha Kolenko

10 9 8 7 6 5 4 3 2 1

First Edition